The
Effective Editor

The Effective Editor

How to Lead Your Staff to Better Writing and Better Teamwork

FOSTER DAVIS AND KAREN F. DUNLAP

The Poynter Institute

and

Bonus Books, Inc.

04 03 02 01 00   5 4 3 2 1

International Standard Book Number: 1-56625-142-7

Library of Congress Control Number: 00-131761

Bonus Books, Inc.

160 East Illinois Street

Chicago, Illinois 60611

www.bonus-books.com

The Poynter Institute

801 Third Street South

St. Petersburg, Florida 33701

www.poynter.org

Table of Contents

ACKNOWLEDGMENTS

To the many editors who toil long hours, inspire staffs, make mistakes, and feel unappreciated, we say thank you.

We are especially grateful to editors who have shaped us.

I, Foster, wish to acknowledge three editors who have taught me much: Hodding Carter III, former editor of the Greenville, MS *Delta Democrat-Times*, Doug Clifton, editor of the *Cleveland Plain Dealer* and Rich Oppel, editor of the Austin, TX *American Statesman*.

I, Karen, wish to acknowledge my first editor, Brad Carlisle of the *Nashville Banner*. He was gruff, forceful, and a stickler for accuracy. After his death, staffers noticed that his name was misspelled in his tombstone. "Brad would have just died," one staffer said. "He would have said, 'My God, it's the last time you write a man's name. Can't you get it right?'"

We are also grateful to the people who allowed us to use their writings, teaching handouts, experiences, etc., in this book. Of special importance is Poynter's Paul Pohlman, wise in the ways of leaders and those who are led.

Our gratitude goes to the *St. Petersburg Times* for the use of re-edited stories as teaching models and to other news organizations for granting permission to use their award-winning stories.

Thanks to all the Poynter people who helped with the production of this book: Roy Peter Clark, Anne Conneen, Priscilla Ely, Betty Headley, Billie Keirstead, Sandy LaDoux, Jim Naughton, Chip Scanlan and David Shedden.

We are especially grateful to our copy editor, Vicki Krueger.

Our deepest gratitude goes to our families.

I, Foster, thank my wife, Cheryl Carpenter, my best editor. I also thank my children, Bradley and Tracy, for withstanding parental editing with good cheer.

I, Karen, thank my husband, Hank, my children, Asim (and Brenda), Christopher (and Donette), Asha, and Justin for being patient. I also thank my grandchildren for being the sunshine in my every day.

PREFACE

This book is primarily for those who work with writers. Our first concern is with news directors, news editors, assigning editors and others who edit journalists. However, we present principles and practices that could help editors of other works: books, public relations presentations, the Internet and many other forms of creative work.

We've designed this as a handbook to help new editors get started and to help experienced editors become better focused. Some of what we say may confirm your practices. Some may challenge them. Try new approaches, and periodically test yourself against goals you set. Keep this little book at hand.

Finally this book has a larger goal, which is to help editors better serve their audiences. Quality journalism engages the public in civic life. Solid news and feature stories help people understand their communities, and equip and inspire people as citizens. Only good journalists can produce such work, and good journalists are the specialty of the effective editor.

INTRODUCTION

Do you remember your first editor?

Most writers do. They treasure memories of the ones they admire, and ridicule those they do not. Writers love editors who stand for something worthwhile, have a passion for compelling writing, and help them grow. They scorn editors who are peevish, unfocused, and generally useless.

Remember how easy it was to judge editors, to criticize and second-guess them? Now you're one.

Few editors come to the job with the skills they need. Most try to look confident while scrambling for direction. They act like the editors they recall and those around them. Feeding the news beast keeps them busy, but doesn't satisfy the urge to do something meaningful. They wonder how to rise from mediocrity to greatness. They wonder how they can become more effective.

Great editors know who they are and what they can achieve. They have a passion for their work. They care about their staffs and focus on first-rate reports for readers, viewers, and listeners. They want to make a difference in the newsroom and, working with others, make a difference in society.

This book is designed to help you get a new grip on editing. New to the job? The first section will help you get started. Been at it for years? Other sections should offer fresh ideas in some areas, confirmation in others.

Before you get started, ask yourself what it takes to be an effective editor. Consider these three sources for answers:

Examples of great editors;
What writers say they need;
Advice from other fields about leadership.

Examples of Great Editors

News people mention great editors with respect as journalists who towered above their peers. Awards and programs bear their names. They were outstanding newsroom leaders with very different styles and achievements. Their actions offer lessons for editors today.

Here are priorities from some of the best.

Improve the Writer

Max Perkins worked with such novelists as Thomas Wolfe, Ernest Hemingway, Marjorie Kinnan Rawlings, and F. Scott Fitzgerald. During 37 years with the House of Scribner he gained the confidence and even the devotion of writers by letting them know he was with them. He said, "You can tell more about a writer by listening to him than by reading something he wrote." By listening, he brought out their best work. One author said Perkins encouraged writers to do what they didn't know they had it in them to do.[1]

---

[1] John Wheelock, ed., *The Letters of Maxwell E. Perkins* (New York: Charles Scribner's Sons, 1987).

Too often editors absorb themselves in improving the story, not the writer. As a result, the story makes deadline and the reporter ends the day frustrated. Editors wonder why writers don't learn from changes made in stories, but many reporters don't review their work because it is no longer their work. Perkins set a different priority. He focused on listening to, encouraging, and improving the writer. Okay, you're thinking, but there are no Scott Fitzgeralds or Marjorie Rawlings on your staff. Perkins' path is still worth following.

Take a Stand

Ida B. Wells looked ahead to prosperity in the late 1880s as her newspaper, the *Free Speech*, gained circulation. But Wells was bothered by injustice. She wrote a series of articles blasting racial prejudice, particularly denouncing lynching in Memphis. A mob burned her newspaper offices to the ground. Wells escaped to the North and became a major voice against injustice through her writing, editing, and speaking.

The world is full of social issues to engage you. Don't shrink from them, although your most important stand might be on issues in your newsroom. Those around you need you to show courage, to stand up for values, to defend good writing. Listen to writers:

"I like editors to challenge those above them when they have bad ideas or unrealistic expectations."

Good editors *"fight for time to do good stories and for space to give them play."*

Those battles might not be glamorous, but they are at the heart of your work.

See the Real Story

Edward R. Murrow brought hard news, fine writing and careful editing to radio and television documentaries. He and co-producer Fred Friendly took a film crew to Korea for television's first full-length combat report; they went to a small community to explore the life of an Air Force officer who had been classified a security risk; and they examined the tactics of McCarthyism. In short, they used the new technology of their time to tell the most important stories in the most compelling ways.[2]

Make Business a Value

"Editor Inc.," an article in a journalism magazine, begins with this statement: "Once upon a time editors ruled their worlds like princes. No more. In today's corporate, high-pressure environment, their roles have multiplied even as their clout has waned." Author Geneva Overholser knows about editors. She was on the editorial board of the *New York Times*, an ombudsman of the *Washington Post*, and as editor of the *Des Moines Register* she led the staff to the Pulitzer Prize for public service. She listed 13 ways of looking at newspaper editors. Among her listings: "money makers," "marketers," and "numbers crunchers."[3]

That's scary stuff, and not just for newspaper editors. The role changes affect almost anyone who edits writers. Yet the problem is

---

[2] Edwin Emery and Michael Emery, *The Press and America*, 1978, p. 406

[3] Geneva Overholser, "Editor, Inc." *American Journalism Review*, December

not new. In the mid-1800s when editor Benjamin Day of the *New York Sun* faced marketing issues, he developed the human interest story. That helped sustain the penny press, thereby launching mass circulation newspapers. The new methods proved the economic value of news.

Your image of the good editor's work might center around crafting award-winning writing, but much of the reality, as you know, is meetings, procedures, reports, and other business matters. Good editors set priorities that give primary attention to developing the writers, but include time to attend to business.

Serve the Community

Carole Kneeland demonstrated how newsroom leaders make a difference. Many local television stations seem to live on the motto, "If it bleeds it leads," the news. Sensational crime coverage builds ratings but lowers credibility. As news director at KVUE-TV, Austin, Texas, Kneeland decided to innovate. She told her newsroom that crime stories had to meet one of five criteria to be aired. They were:

The crime had to pose an immediate threat;
The crime had to pose a threat to children;
The crime had to warrant some response by the public;
The crime had to have significant impact;
The broadcast had to aid in crime prevention efforts.

"Life is too short to worry about taking some risks," she said. "If the thing I became known for was getting fired because I tried to reduce the amount of senseless, violent crime on the station, that's okay with me."

Under her leadership KVUE became the top station in its market.

What Writers Say They Need

Famous editors can inspire, but you don't think of the greats most days. You do think about the people you hear from every day — the reporters. In the hassle of editing stories and making dead-lines, it's easy to hear, but not really listen. Listen now to five suggestions by reporters who responded to a question on how editors could better help them:

Communicate With Us

"Tell me when I do a good job. And when I don't quite hit the mark, tell me that too."

You work in a communications field, but too often you don't communicate. The pressure of time, an unwillingness to be direct, the inability to explain changes meaningfully, and the habit of fixing rather than coaching all hinder communication. In addition, you may be separated by distance and time, making it hard to talk.

Your writers need response from their first and best audience: you. Keep it short, make it specific. You needn't gush, but recognize good work, and don't ignore weaknesses. The goal is to improve the writer, who will improve the story.

Work With Us, Not Against Us

"The best editors I've had were collaborators. It was never, 'My way or the highway.' It was, 'Let's talk about this.' "

The image of the writer is of a lone figure hammering away. The image of the editor is of the sage wordsmith making decisive changes. The reality is that the two need to work together. Writers and editors work in an organization, which means they work with other people. Their best work, most of the time, will be done in association with those colleagues.

Trust and Respect Us

"I appreciate an editor who trusts me when I say a story on my beat is, or isn't, important."

"I work closely with three editors and most of the time my editors don't help me. About the most positive thing I can say for one of them is that she helps me focus ideas. I can talk with that editor because she treats me with a modicum of respect and trust."

Walter Lippman wrote that reality for us is "the pictures in our heads." One of the more difficult leaps of the human psyche is to release the picture in the editor's head to the reality of the scribe who has been on the scene. True, the scribe has to be trustworthy. As an editor, you must show writers the standards for trust and help them achieve those standards.

Defend Good Work

"They will lobby for better play on stories we believe in. That's a real plus."

An editor is a shepherd, helping writers get good stories into the paper, guarding the stories from being shorn of their individuality.

Become the Voice for Good Writing in Our Heads

"Editors force clarifications, precision, and tighter, better writing. They are the mother in your head, nagging you to check the facts. A good editor will make you even better than you are."

You won't, can't, and shouldn't always be with your writers. But your words about good writing can be, and should be. Your job is to work yourself out of a job, by helping writers to develop the habits that make for complete and satisfying stories.

Advice from Other Fields about Leadership

Much of what makes you an effective editor is simply leadership. Here are some thoughts on improving leadership.

Peter Drucker based his classic, *The Effective Executive,* on five practices. He said leaders, like you, need to:

Know where your time goes. Chart your days and see where you really devote your time and energy, then make the needed changes;

Focus on the significant contribution that you want to make. Ask, "What can I do that will significantly affect this company?";

Build on the strengths of those you work with. Play to the strengths of superiors, direct those you supervise to their strengths;

Make a few major tasks your priorities. You can choose to do many things poorly, or a few things well;

Make effective decisions. Watch for the important opportunities and decide wisely.

Among the *Seven Habits of Highly Successful People,* Stephen Covey noted the need to:

Be proactive. Get ahead of a situation, don't wait to respond;

Begin with a goal in mind. Establish your personal principles of leadership;

Put first things first. Don't spend the day putting out fires. Instead, do what is most important;

Learn to work with people. That means taking the time to figure out others;

Find time to renew. Get a life outside the job.

Public Radio journalists produced a guidebook on independence and integrity in which they called on news directors to focus on:

Vision: the knowledge of where the organization should be headed and how to get there;

Communication: the ability to describe that vision to people and get them to "buy into" it as well as giving them a role in decisions;

Insight: a knack for evaluating talent, solving problems and generating innovative ideas; and

Commitment: reflecting concern for listeners and staff.

These lists are similar, aren't they? The common characteristics are setting priorities and goals, getting to know your company, getting to know your people and letting them get to know you, having common goals and building on strength rather than shoring up weakness.

What Do You Need to Do?

We have explored three paths in answering the question, "What makes a great editor?" We noted the qualities of outstanding editors, the skills that reporters seek in editors, and the characteristics of good leadership. Notice the similarities. Certain traits stand out in each group. Let's use them to describe the qualities we seek. Good editors:

Understand themselves and their roles. They have arrived at a sense of mission about their work that guides them. They have a passion for the task that gives them energy. They set priorities and let those guide their daily work.

Understand their power. The real power is not in the title, but in the ability to influence people. They invest time in learning about the people with whom they work. They listen, focus on their strengths, communicate effectively and build trust.

Continually sharpen their craft skills. They constantly improve their ability to see and improve stories. They develop the language to discuss stories and become teachers to those they edit.

Grow as leaders. You must lead. That means giving directions and making sure they are followed, seeing that processes are carried out effectively, talking straight during evaluations, handling conflict, and conducting yourself professionally even when everything falls apart. It means constantly learning to be a leader.

Those four areas are the topics of the sections in this book:

Getting Started;
The Editor's Power;
Craft Skills for the Long Run;
Leadership Skills for Today and Tomorrow.

Take your time, read the book, try out the practices suggested. Use it as your guide to ways of evaluating your work. Let it be a source of new ideas and approaches. Your investment in becoming a better editor could determine how your staff remembers you. Those reporters again:

"Editors are subject to far greater pressures from above than reporters are, and get fewer compliments for their work, but what they do is absolutely vital."

"A good editor is a gem to treasure forever."

Section I
Getting Started

CHAPTER ONE
The First Year

To become an editor is to choose a difficult but rewarding life. Keep those rewards in mind, for the difficulties have a way of impressing themselves upon you, year after year, but especially in your first year. If you feel unprepared for your new role, you can at least take comfort in the company you are in.

In broadcast and newspaper newsrooms we are familiar with, in the United States, Scandinavia and Africa, most new editors are thrust into the job with scant preparation. If you are in the typical situation, you will learn by doing. You will mishandle a writer and sense the chill in the air. You will look at the raw copy of your former colleagues and realize that those editors — now your colleagues — were not simply waving other people's work into print or onto the air. You will become the "someone" people are referring to when they say, "Someone ought to do something about that."

So, how to begin? First, understand that you really have chosen a different kind of work. Being good at your former work of reporting and writing is good, but insufficient to assure your success. Your new work is to get things done through other people — those talented and notoriously cranky and self-absorbed people who are drawn into the writing life.

The skills that served you as a writer are inadequate for an editor. They are very useful, but they don't go far enough. Your skills as a reporter and as a writer are important, so long as you understand that you are no longer either, and so long as you don't pine too much for your former life.

Your own ability to write a good story is no longer the test. The challenge now is to aid and abet others in doing good work. You need to make a plan and use it. Here is why. Nearly everyone will want you to do well in a new job, but whether you actually do well is mostly up to you.

This is scary, but liberating. It means you understand that your success is in your hands. By the way, there are few things more comforting to a seasoned editor than seeing a new editor diligently trying to understand her new craft, and sticking with it. You want to be that kind of a new editor, and a plan will help you.

We are talking about a plan for your first year. A useful way to think of that year is the first three days, the first three weeks, and the first three months. Why these time periods? In three days, you have worked the better part of a typical workweek, but it is not too late to make changes that will have impact in that first week. In three weeks, you have worked the better part of a month, with time to make changes in that month. And three months seems to be about the amount of time people typically require to get acclimated to a new job. Also, three months is the time customarily allotted for a probationary period for new employees.

This rule of three invites you to think dispassionately about what and how you are doing. Imagine that it is the Sunday evening before you begin your new job, although real life is rarely so tidy. You are sitting in a quiet corner with a notebook and pen.

Like any reasonable person about to start supervising writers, you are nervous. Here is where some systematic thought can pay off. Here is where you develop your plan.

First, *review yourself*. What do you know, and what do you need to know? What skills and qualities do you bring to the job? And — let's be blunt — what are your weaknesses, and what will you do about them? You may have a pretty good idea about these things. The questions people threw at you as you interviewed for the job may have helped you see yourself as others see you. That is valuable, up to a point, but it is no substitute for honest introspection.

Honest means honest. It does not mean flagellating yourself because you don't know all you wish you did, and it does not mean you must assume all your motives are ignoble. Or noble, for that matter. So, on this mythical Sunday evening, cool drink at hand, ask yourself some questions you've asked before.

Why do I want to be an editor?

Because more money comes with the job.
Because I like the title of assistant editor, or news director, or creative director, or producer.
Because I want to get my hand on the wheel.
Because I have teaching and coaching skills.
Because I like to help journalists.

This last reason is important, although the others are not to be sneered at. Much of the satisfaction in editing comes from helping journalists to improve. Does this seem to contradict the hoary notion of the timeless editor whose bite is as bad as his bark? Perhaps so, but in the real world such editors are rarely effective. As we will see, a mental toughness is essential, but tough-guy histrionics are not. Moreover, they will deny you one of an editor's best rewards, which is the sense of approval from the people being edited. This is not a matter of playing to the crowd, or worrying overmuch about displeasing the people you supervise. If you aren't making them angry from time to time, you are probably being timid, which will also anger them.

The general approval of writers matters. Unless there is response to your leadership, you won't be very effective. Editors ultimately preside with the consent of the governed. You can rule a sullen newsroom, but it is hard to get it to do very much.

Editors succeed based in good measure on that unspoken plebiscite from the floor. Good editors attract writers, and they get better work out of them — and more of it — than the writers think they can produce. Good editors help writers improve. No editor builds a decent life on failing writers. So think about why you want to be an editor. Money and title are not enough. Power is not enough, although it is something.

So, why do you want to be an editor?

The best answer we know to that question would be something like this: "Because I like showing people how to do better work, and watching them get better. I don't get a byline, or my name on the air, but I have a hand in much of what we do."

That is the answer that will keep you going during the tough times. That is the answer that means editing can make you happy. It does not mean, though, the people you supervise will be happy, so on this mythical Sunday evening ask yourself the second question.

What skills do I have and which ones can I apply immediately? (By immediately, we mean tomorrow morning.)

I am a good reporter.

I write well, and others respect my work.

I deal with sources like a grownup.

I am well organized.

I have good news judgment.

I spout ideas for taking stories and news coverage beyond the routine.

I can articulate story ideas in ways that inform and persuade my colleagues.

I have enough energy to stay on the case, and enough humor to keep it fun, at least much of the time.

If all of that is true, you're over-qualified. We know of very few editors who could honestly claim all those qualities when they began as editors. You don't need them all, either, at least not to make a good start. You do need some of them, and you have them, or you wouldn't be making the leap into editing.

You do need the most honest assessment you are capable of making. That's why this review of your skills is important. Look at yourself sympathetically, but realistically. Write down what you see. What's missing? What's going to cause you problems? What do you need to work on first?

High on any reasonable list would be being organized. We stress this because on a lot of days, regardless of your organizational skills, your editing life is likely to feel like being caught up in boiling surf, tossed about for hours and then, miraculously, being thrown onto the beach at the end of the day, gasping but alive.

This happens partly for reasons you understand: News, at least part of it, is what we didn't know about yesterday, and because it is happening right now we must react.

It happens partly for reasons you'll eventually accept but never understand: For example, the publisher always, from your perspective, picks the worst time to demand information and documentation about last month's overtime.

If you don't have a basic sense of organization going into such days, you'll accomplish very little, and you're likely to feel like a pingpong ball in a room full of fans. In the next chapter, we'll look at how to develop, and improve, those organizational skills.

On this Sunday evening, though, we are looking at the next three days, so you will get a good start on your new editing life.

If you start with a few useful practices in those first days, you'll assure yourself that whatever other gaffes you commit, you will have done a few good things in your first week. You will feel as though you have some control over your new job.

Make habits of these tasks from your first day, and they will support you every day thereafter. They will help you develop a routine so that certain things take care of themselves. Then you'll be left with the brain space to handle the surf.

Do these five things from your first day:

1. Keep a calendar, and write things down. Anticipate dates — evaluations, anniversaries, birthdays.
2. Keep a to-do list. Revise it at the end of each day.
3. Get to work early. Coming in late means you start your day   feeling a little off-balance.
4. Learn about the people who work for you. What are they good at? What could they be better at? What drives them? Their effectiveness is the key to your success.
5. Spend some time, daily, walking around asking people how they're doing, what they're working on. Editors often feel

awkward doing this. Persist. It will become more comfortable. Don't subconsciously avoid people with whom you feel no rapport.

If you will do these five things from the start, that start will be a decent one.

A decent start is critical because high among your management tasks is managing your own confidence. The change from writer to editor, from line to supervision, is profound. Many a writer-turned-editor has discovered he just doesn't like being in charge. In fact, diffidence toward their own authority is a key reason why editors fail. They simply will not accept their authority. And even if you do accept your authority, you are likely to exercise it awkwardly for a while. You need to do at least some things right. Lists and calendars will help.

Be prepared to feel off-balance a lot of the time in your first weeks. Ask for help from more experienced editors in setting priorities. Get a superior, or an experienced colleague, to debrief you daily on what you are doing well, and not so well. You simply must have a lot of information.

It takes most people about three months to get over that initial feeling of disorientation. You will experience some typical editing squeezes. The layout desk pleads for shorter stories; the reporters plead for more space and you are expected to reconcile the conflict, keep peace in the family, and hit your deadlines. Night after night. And manage the weekend schedule, and keep track of the spending, year to date.

You will wonder why you are working so hard, and wonder if it will ever become fun. This is, more or less, normal. Editing really is a different life. If you persist, you'll gradually start experiencing some of the satisfactions. You'll do some things right in those first months. Some things will go better than you expected.

Do the basic things right, listen to the people you work for and who work for you, and behave so that your grandmother would be proud. That will get you through your first year better than most.

CHAPTER TWO
Get Organized and Stay That Way

As an editor, the stakes are higher for you now. A disorganized writer mostly hurts herself, although there's surely some impact on her overall contributions to her organization.

Once you accept responsibility for the performance of others, though, your efficiency matters in a new way. A disorganized editor hampers the work of anyone around her. She no doubt has many good qualities. It's just that you cannot be certain that if she says something will be done it will be done. She may have lost her list, or she may never have written down what she agreed to get done, and in the day's busyness she forgot about it.

Here are two simple rules:

Do what you say you're going to do.

Be where you say you're going to be.

People need to be able to count on you. You need to be able to count on yourself. And that requires you to be reasonably well organized.

Reasonably. There is such a thing as being too organized, so that organization itself becomes the product. You don't need that.

You need some organization, which amounts to making good use of your time. Being organized is about time. For an editor, it is not just your time but the time of people around you.

Organization gives you more time by helping you waste less of it. Sounds obvious, but many editors lament their lack of time, while wasting it. You can learn to be reasonably well organized just as you can learn to iron a shirt or change a tire or surf the web. It is a skill, or a set of skills.

So what is it to be organized? It is not neatness; it is not a clean desktop. Getting organized is about developing certain habits, nothing more. It is simply this: a habit of categorizing all that comes before you and placing materials where the logic of the categories suggests.

You categorize in two ways: by topic and by time. Our brains are constantly trying to assign categories to help us make sense of our world. So, to make sense of your work life, you need to help your brain do what it is predisposed to do: organize what's around it in a way that helps it understand.

This frees your brain to concentrate on the work itself. Compared with how your work life may now feel, it gives you improved control.

So don't listen to that little voice that says you're just disorganized. You can learn to do this just as you learned any skill. You learned to drive, didn't you? This is just one more thing to learn.

Three Basic Tools

You will use a calendar, a notebook, and a file drawer.

It may seem odd that in this computerized age we lean so heavily on pencil and paper. We like computers and the personal organizing programs that work with them. Also, handheld devices keep getting better. One of us uses one; one does not. One of us uses a computer-based organizer, one does not. But we both use paper calendars, notebooks and manila folders.

Start with the pre-electronic stuff, and graduate to the computer or the handheld device when you have a paper-based system that works.

Think about how you actually do your work. Are you mostly at your desk? Or do you roam your newsroom, chatting with this reporter, that producer, that online editor? Should your calendar and notebook always be with you? The beauty of having them at your desk is that they are always there. Yet people in fast-moving organizations often make lots of on-the-fly decisions — lunch next Tuesday, read the draft of Jack's story before 5, the publisher wants to talk tomorrow about a regional edition — based on encounters with people they bump into on their way to do something else.

But if you cannot conveniently carry your calendar and notebook, you may find yourself setting them down here and there, then wasting time looking for them. Decide what works for you and use it consistently.

Whatever you wind up with, your tools should be portable enough to travel home and out of town with you. So don't make a desk calendar your main calendar.

Visit an office supply store. Is there a date book that can combine the functions of calendar and notebook? After all, your notebook and calendar are things you will turn to, literally, dozens of times a day. If the heart of your organizing effort can exist in a single item, so much the better.

If you buy something and then find it doesn't serve you well, replace it. The expense is trivial compared with the benefit. Get things you will use.

Get a box of 100 letter-sized manila file folders, with tabs to the left, right and center. Do your cuticles a favor and get the heavy-duty kind where the tab side is folded over. Leave the legal-sized folders to the lawyers. You want to be able to keep some of these things on your desk without covering it.

Get several fiber-tipped marking pens, in different colors, for labeling your files.

Lay in a supply of 3 by 3 sticky notes.

How to Use Them

First, use your calendar, your notebook, and your files daily. Write things down, consistently. When something strikes you, jot it down in your notebook. When you agree to do something, jot it down in your calendar. When you start a new project, open a file.

The power is in consistency, although you won't do this perfectly. You are bound to write something in your calendar that really belongs in your notebook, and vice versa. You still have only two places to look: your calendar and your notebook.

Your Calendar

In your new calendar, enter all the items for the year ahead that you can. You are a supervisor, so presumably you are responsible for annual evaluations, for example. Note those dates, and enter a reminder to begin preparing several weeks beforehand. When that date comes up, start. Even if you just gather materials and create a manila folder for the task, you'll have made a start. We will have more to say later about evaluations.

Be inclusive with your calendar. That writing conference six months from now that you'd like two of your people to attend. The date that school resumes, Christmas vacation begins, graduation takes place. When people want to take vacations. In the aggregate, these entries will help you see when things will be at their most hectic.

If you are using a shirt-pocket sized calendar and you find yourself running out of room, add space where you need it with sticky notes.

When you can see all these things written into your calendar, you'll get that first comforting feeling of having achieved some control.

You may want to jot down what seem to be significant moments, thus creating a bit of a diary. It is also a good place to note reimbursable expenses. Every so often, take a few minutes and page through your calendar. Notice how you are using your time.

Your Notebook

The first rule for an editor's notebook is the same as the first rule for an editor's calendar: Use it. Begin each day with a list of those things you intend to get done. End each day by writing your list for the next day.

Write ideas down, notes from meetings, obligations, anything at all. Writing things down organizes you, partly because it creates a record, partly because writing stimulates thought.

Your Files

The manila file folder is a marvelous organizing device. At the most basic level, filing is simply this: You put like things together in one folder, label the folder boldly so you can identify it at a glance, and then keep it at hand.

However, a few refinements will help.

So here is a way to file. If you are an assistant features or city editor or associate news director, this should manage the files you would ordinarily accumulate. If your filing needs are larger, this approach will scale up fairly easily. Start sorting your papers. You will start seeing patterns. A big pattern: Paper that requires action versus paper that does not. Have a pile labeled To-Do. Have another pile labeled Toss. All other papers go into a filing category.

As papers appear that suggest a category (city hall, project ideas, hot job prospects, professional meetings, training), jot a category name on a 3 by 5 card. Place one by each pile of paper.

When you're done, you're likely to have at least 20 labeled piles.

Now think about whether the label makes sense, based on the overview that the sorting has given you. Label each folder in two places, on the tab and across the end. That way you can keep a dozen or more folders you use constantly laid out like fallen dominoes, and read their labels at a glance.

It takes only a few seconds to open a drawer and pull out a file. But if you do that five or 10 times a day you will weary of it. Hence, your heavily used files deserve a ready-access position on some of your precious desk space.

Your file labels are topical. Within each folder, absent any other organization, arrange the papers chronologically, the newest materials on top. You might decide to subdivide some folders. If you are working on a project and have some correspondence, some meeting notes about the original goals, and some source materials, you might decide to keep the three segments separated, with paper clips. Organize the papers held by each paper clip chronologically, unless some other organization makes sense.

The point is simplicity and consistency, so you don't have to think much about it. Use common sense. If you have a total of 12 papers in a file, you do not need subgroups. You want reasonably ready access, without allowing the filing process to consume much time.

If you have a lot of files, consider organizing them into four to six categories. One might be "People." That could include material on staffers and people you might hire. Another category might be "Administrivia," for the various administrative matters you handle. A third might be "Projects." If this feels unnecessary, don't bother.

Any file you use a lot belongs on your desk.

We suggest you have an individual file for each person you supervise. When someone does something well, toss a note into the file. When something concerns you, toss a note into the file. Over time, such a file will give you a closer view of the person you supervise, and you will write a far more astute evaluation, if your company does them.

Create a file each time you start some new enterprise. You can always throw it away. If you keep materials in your computer, label them exactly as your paper files are labeled.

Your object is to be able to lay hands on any materials, real or virtual, within a minute or two. Working as we've described, you'll be able to.

Finally, that innovation of the 1980s, the sticky note.

Use them like this:

For a day in your calendar or day book where there's more to say than the space available, add space by attaching sticky notes to the day. Start an idea on a sticky note in your notebook, move it to the calendar as appropriate, or to the inside of a file folder.

Carry some sticky notes in your notebook or even in the fold of a wallet (10 are the thickness of a credit card). Use them as quick notes, to be transferred to files, calendar, or another person as appropriate.

At the end of your workday, spend 3 to 5 minutes reviewing your calendar, to-do list, and files. Put files away if you think you are through with them, on your desk or in the drawer. Note what's on your calendar, what's in your notebook, and transfer any information that seems appropriate. Write a new to-do list for tomorrow. Take your materials home, if that's what you do, or leave them on your desk, if that's what you do.

Relax.

A Final Note

If you consider yourself poorly organized, have some patience with your progress. To form a constructive new habit is a struggle. Allow three months of daily attentiveness for a new habit to take hold. Reinforce the changes you are making. Tape a short list to the edge of your computer screen if that helps. It might say:

1. Write it down.
2. Daily to-do list.
3. Use the calendar.
4. Use the files.
5. Write it down.

Section II
The Editor's Power

CHAPTER THREE
Your Ambiguous Power

The early morning caller sounded cheerful and casual. As he introduced himself, we tried to place him. He said he was an assistant city editor with a couple of problems, and wondered if we'd heard how others solved them. First, he had a senior reporter who once excelled but now turned in drab stories. He also had a promising young reporter who left holes in her work. Facts were missing or wrong. She came with good clips after two years in another newsroom, but she wasn't measuring up.

"I feel like changing jobs or going back to drinking," he said. We laughed. "Why not talk to the veteran," we suggested, "find out what he wants to do, what would motivate him?" He'd done that. The veteran wanted to do long take-out pieces, stories that didn't fit in the newspaper's plan. Why not coach the young reporter on her errors? Take them step by step. He had, but she didn't get it. She made the same mistakes over and over, forcing him to rewrite.

His problems reached beyond the two reporters. What did his editor say? Nothing. His editor was always in meetings and just said "deal with" the problem cases. Was it time to think of moving the reporters or firing them? "No way," he said. Company tradition and fear of legal actions meant the two weren't going anywhere. "I wasn't kidding," the caller said, his voice much slower and deeper. "I feel like leaving the industry or going back to drinking."

Power isn't always what we think it is.

Too often we imagine that the powerful newsroom leader mimics Lou Grant, who ruled his domain. When he stormed into the newsroom all eyes turned to him. He growled and everyone jumped. He gave orders and the staff obeyed, and seldom did higher-ups trouble him.

Chances are things don't work that way for you, just as they weren't that way for the caller.

You are constantly in a squeeze play. You must retain your dignity despite second-guessing from bosses and reporters. You risk having your news judgments contradicted and your editing lapses highlighted. You wanted to be an editor to inspire great journalism. Instead you sometimes see yourself in a job that offers little intellectual stimulation and is emotionally draining.

Where is the power in all this? Remember, as an editor you have the opportunity to make a difference in your newsroom. This chapter suggests that you take a new look at power. Examine four areas of strength. You can:

Focus on your purpose;
Find the forms of power that suit you;
Decide on your limits;
Discover your assets in the newsroom.

Consider each to get away from your forlorn thoughts, and into effective leadership.

Focus on Your Purpose

Remember the story of the man in a cave? He won great battles by conquering enemies who far outnumbered him. He stood for his beliefs and won, but then a new threat appeared and he ran away, dejected, to hide in a cave. As he sulked, the voice from on high came to him asking: "What are you doing here?"

The question wasn't to scold; it was a reminder about mission. Why had the man fought? Why was he now in a cave? What changed his mission? Things weren't out of control; the man just allowed himself to believe they were. A reminder about his mission got him out the funk and back in the battle.

Regularly remind yourself of your purpose as a journalist. Recall your strengths, and build on them. Keep check on your weaknesses. Struggle to overcome them. Keep before you the ways in which you can make a difference and act on them.

Find the Forms of Power that Suit You

Paul Pohlman of The Poynter Institute and members of the Human Resources Center at the University of Chicago have described five types of power.[4]

---

[4] List developed by Paul Pohlman of The Poynter Institute and members of the University of Chicago Human Resources Center, based on three works: "The Bases of Social Power" by John R.P French and Bertram Raven in *Group Dynamics*, 2nd ed., ed. Dorwin Cartwright and A.F. Zaner (Evanston, IL.: Row, Peterson, 1960); "Power Failure in Management Circuits," by Rosebeth Moss Kaner in *Harvard Business Review*, July-August 1979; and *Power and Influence* by John R. Kotter, The Free Press, 1985.

Legitimate power. This is the formal position that we so often think of as the only source of power. It seems so authoritative, efficient, and impressive. Power comes through appointment that brings a title, responsibility, and a domain. The implication is that one needs only to act and others will respond accordingly. The military makes legitimate power clear to a recruit. Within three weeks the drill instructor turns a clueless trainee into an expert on the chain of command. She is able to make distinctions based on stripes on the arm and medals on the shoulder. In any situation she knows who is in charge of what, how to respond to orders, and what to expect if she doesn't respond appropriately.

As editor, you have rank, but don't expect the stripes alone to inspire enthusiastic compliance. Many people don't respond well to orders. Journalists rank high on this anti-authoritarian list. They want to be inspired, convinced, encouraged, but not commanded. The stripes do give a good foundation. You'll have some sense of your territory of control and a megaphone allowing you to be heard. These are important in gridlock and on deadline. Otherwise, you'll spend a good deal of time relying on other sources of power.

Expert power. Look around your newsroom and think about the people who command respect because of what they know. Look more widely around the company and think of the folks who are indispensable, even though they don't have ranking titles. They are essential because of what they can do. Others approach them because they need their help.

In the quiet recesses of the *St. Petersburg Times* news library, Debbie Wolfe caught the hint of a wave. She moved from being a deskless "clip puller" to news researcher by designing a unique study of journalism and the growing number of computer research services. Next she became a resource for reporters, by showing them how to find new sources online. From there she began teaching online reporting skills and started to plan training programs for the newsroom. The more she did, the more she found to do. Her job title changed to Technology Training Editor, and at that point she had gained official power. Notice, though, that the title followed her newly acquired expertise. She gained power and position because of what she learned.

Expert power can cut two ways for an editor. You ought to have a store of craft knowledge that allows you to help writers improve, but editors trip on being too expert. They become know-it-alls who spout answers when they ought to be listening, and they make changes when a few key questions would help the reporter grow. The ideal is to improve your knowledge constantly. Then you will draw others to you because of what you know and the manner in which you help them grow.

Trade-off power. People gain power through their ability to provide the things that others need. While it smells of sleaze, of wheeling and dealing, it can be the pivotal factor in your success or frustration. Trade-off calls on you to get to know supervisors and other staffers well enough to provide what they need to meet their goals. It also involves your well-thought-out response to those who are diligent and to those who regularly give less than their best.

Consider your trade-off power. You wield perks and penalties. Use them fairly and wisely and you are a fine leader. Show partiality or overreact, and the newsroom loses respect for you. Use them haphazardly and you've wasted them. Don't use them at all and you'll see the staff ignoring your directions. You'll be among the mass of editors who moan about reporters regularly missing deadlines.

The perks you offer begin with a sincere thank you for a job well done. They move on to a casual show of gratitude spoken loudly enough for others to hear, to choice assignments, better story play, and your all-out effort for monetary rewards. Think of the other perks available for you to trade.

The penalties are equally important: a private word of disappointment such as, "I know you can do better," a clear written evaluation that spells out areas to improve, or a reluctance to entrust prized story assignments until weaknesses are addressed.

Trade-offs work with supervisors, too. Healthy relations develop when people work together toward the same goal. Implicit in that is a trade-off: "Since we're working toward the same end, if you help me toward my goal, I'll help you toward yours." Invest the time in knowing what your supervisors and colleagues are trying to achieve and look for opportunities that serve all.

Differences can complicate the trade-off process. It takes effort to look beyond differences in style, background, gender, race, ethnic group, and sexual orientation, but you can and should overcome divisions.

Paula Madison took the challenge. She's vice president of news at WNBC-TV, New York City. An incident during her teen years affected her sense of news. Growing up in Harlem, Madison witnessed a major police shoot-out, but none of the news outlets reported it. Years later as a reporter, she chafed at the white, middle-class orientation of her station's news coverage. One day she asked her news director to take a short tour of the city with her. They started on a subway, and her supervisor noticed there was no air conditioning. That was his first lesson on how his morning commute in a fine car differed from the experiences of many in the city. By the end of the tour, the two were talking about ways to broaden the station's view of city life. Madison took a risk in approaching her boss, but the trade-off was better understanding, and better news coverage.

Referent power. When the reporter was a child, she was frustrated by the complexity of the English language. There were too many rules, and too many exceptions to them. Her mother taught English, but Mom's explanations seemed mysterious, too. Still, Mom's example helped. When the child found a question she couldn't answer, she'd think, "How would Momma say this?" She usually got it right.

In most businesses you find a few people whose behavior makes them models for others. They gain power through example. People gravitate to them for advice, or emulate them from afar. Referent power is similar to expert power, but there is a difference. We often admire the expert knowledge, without wanting to imitate the experts. Referent power flows from personal qualities that lead to respect.

Years after his death, Jim Millstone's pictures could still be found in the *St. Louis Post-Dispatch* newsroom. He had been an outstanding reporter and then assistant managing editor. He was a tough editor. High praise from him amounted to this: "I see no major problem with your story." Millstone sought excellence in each story. He sought to help interns and young staffers. He cared about his staff. When one reporter, worried about her mother's health, was struggling with a big story, Millstone told her to go home and relax. The story was important, but the person was more important.

Millstone had formal power, and he was an expert on stories, but his real power grew out of the respect others had for him.

Do others seek to model you? If they did, what qualities would they emulate? What type of conduct would you see?

Value power. This power comes from a person who exhibits strong values that are shared by others. Mahatma Gandhi, Martin Luther King Jr., and Mother Teresa gained influence because of their commitment to certain values. That power is found in news organizations, too.

Editors who worked with Nelson Poynter tell of his approach in teaching the value of readers. Periodically he'd request a change in some aspect of the *St. Petersburg Times,* maybe in design or in the type of coverage. A staffer would explain the difficulties that the change would cause. After listening patiently, Poynter would pull a dime from his pocket and say, "Here's my dime. I'm the reader. Get it done." His appeal was not to his power as publisher, but to his commitment to readers, to do whatever was required to serve them. Editors responded by finding a way to make the changes, by remembering the importance of the reader, and by finding jars to save the dimes.

Power comes from being faithful to values in times of testing. Millstone valued accuracy and would hold a story until he was sure the report was true. Could you do that? In the face of competition from online, print, and broadcast news can you uphold the value of accuracy? News leaders wrestle with infotainment, trash news, and dumbing down the news. Do you have clear values about what is fit to print or produce? Can you explain and defend your stance? Ultimately, leadership is about forming, explaining, and maintaining values. Where do you stand?

These, then, are five types of power available to you. Each gives you a means to achieve goals, and each carries a price. There is a consequence to relying on official power; there is a cost to earning respect for your values. The five have an effect singularly or in combination. Before re-assessing your use of these tools, consider this mini-case study in the use of power:

An award-winning news story profiled a school superintendent who was on the verge of losing his job. He cared about students and was passionate about helping them succeed in school. He understood the classroom since he had been a teacher, and continued to refer to himself as a teacher. He was a man of high moral standards. Even those who opposed him respected his character and considered him above reproach. He worked hard, often working days that began at 6 a.m., and continued through late night meetings. He sacrificed time with his wife and son to be sure he was on top of his work. He had a clear vision for turning a struggling system around. He had sought the job for years because he was confident that his plan could make a big difference.

Although he spoke of his vision, others weren't clear about it. Even some of his top assistants only had a glimmer of what he was trying to achieve. He hated the politics of the job. He didn't spend time with officials whose decisions affected his district and his job. When he was in formal meetings with them, he didn't speak up. He was a big man with a resonant voice, but his style wasn't to inject himself vigorously in these types of conversations. He believed his work spoke for him. He was also hesitant about confronting weak supervisors, especially principals. He was strong as a mentor, but less effective in correcting employees who needed to improve. Over time, his supporters weakened in defending him. As he came under attack, he grew weary of the battle.

How would you evaluate his use of power? In what areas was he strong, and where was he weak? What advice would you give him? Now consider your own use of power. Write two paragraphs on your leadership habits. How would others describe your practices? Where can you go to get an objective report on your conduct? What advice would you give yourself? What are your strengths? Where do you need to improve?

Decide on Your Limits

You will be tempted to be all things to all people: friend to old friends, good soldier to the boss, problem solver for HR staff, wise voice to your community, savior to your writers, and god-like figure to rookie reporters. Yield to the temptation, and you will serve none of them well. An editor wears many hats. David Boardman, an editor at the *Seattle Times*, listed "20 Hats of a Great Editor" (next page) demonstrating that you will need to tap your life skills as much as your craft skills.

You will be stretched, but before you're stretched too thin, give thought to your limits. What are your unyielding principles and what will you negotiate? You will be called on to defend your reporters. How far should you go? Co-workers will come to you with personal problems. When does providing a sympathetic ear become a full-time job as a psychiatrist? How do you avoid becoming a crutch? Many new leaders find the biggest challenge is their relationship with friends they now supervise. Invariably your friendship will change. You have confidences that you can't share and you approach each other from different positions. Accept the change, but respect the friends. As you develop new colleagues at a different level, strive for a healthy connection with old friends.

Finally, let's talk about the sandwich in which you find yourself. Your reporters press from one side, management presses from the other. The only way to avoid being squished is to maintain your character. Decide which battles you'll fight. You can't fight them all and you'll lose effectiveness if you tackle everything with the same fervor. Decide what things you will fight for and how you will fight. Will your style focus on outrage or negotiation? When should you change your style? You won't know the answer for many situations until they arise, but think through processes that will guide your reactions. One of the first rules of martial arts is to take a balanced stance. When you're balanced you can move in any direction quickly and with power. Don't let the world squeeze you. Stay firm, keep your balance, choose your battles wisely, and fight valiantly.

THE 20 HATS OF A GREAT EDITOR
How to be a full-service editor instead of a fixer

REPORTER: *You must be a journalist in your heart and soul. If you haven't been a reporter, even for a year or two, go be one. And even as an editor, there's plenty of opportunity to help your reporters out with a little reporting. While the reporters are talking to sources, surf the Web for good background information for them. Even if you don't have a direct hand in the reporting of a story, you can play reporter with your reporters. Be curious. Ask them questions. Most importantly, show plenty of interest in what they're doing.*

COACH: *Don't be Woody Hayes or Bobby Knight; don't throw chairs or punch your reporters. Be Phil Jackson, when he coached the Chicago Bulls, or Gary Barnett, when he guided the resurgence of Northwestern football. A good coach puts players in the right position for their skills, clearly lays out expectations, provides the necessary tools and guidance, shoulders blame for failures and is free with praise for successes.*

TEACHER: *When you offer advice, do so in a way that helps*

your reporter take away something to use in the future. Watch for patterns — too much reliance on passive verbs, too few quotes, imprecise language — and use those to teach.

STUDENT: *Respect what your reporters know, and what you can learn from them. Let them know you're open to learning, and don't try to pretend you know things you don't. Develop a symbiotic student/teacher relationship that works both ways.*

PSYCHIATRIST: *Learn what makes your reporters tick. Some need a deadline to be productive; others get too nervous under pressure. Some need constant consultation and re-assurance; others like to be left alone. Understanding them and their motivations will help you help them.*

MAESTRO: *Think of the story as a song and yourself as the orchestra conductor. It is possible to edit extensively, to leave your own mark on rhythm and pacing of a story if that's necessary, and still to respect and retain the reporter's melody. You know which words and phrases reflect extra thought and effort on the reporter's part; if they work, keep your grubby hands off them. Hone your ear by reading good writing aloud.*

READER: *Read, read, read whatever you can get your hands on. Other newspapers, magazines and Internet lists for story ideas. Nonfiction for story ideas and research methods. Fiction for literary strategies and character development. Mystery novels for narrative techniques.*

LIBRARIAN: *When you find great stories elsewhere, share them with your reporters. Do the same with books.*

DIPLOMAT: *When you have to say something the reporter would rather not hear about a story, say it gracefully. Focus first on what works, then on what doesn't. And use precise, helpful language. "Can you think of a specific example to make your point clearer to the read-*

ers?" for example. Not, "This lead sucks."

PHOTO EDITOR: *As much as you might implore your reporters to think about pictures to go with their stories, chances are they won't give it proper attention. And no matter how strong your photo staff, you're more likely to get the right pictures with your stories if you're heavily involved. You shouldn't step on the real photo editors' toes, of course, but you should freely suggest photos that capture the essence of the story or provide information best communicated through photography.*

GRAPHICS EDITOR: *Again, you should be constantly thinking about what information can be presented graphically. Often, in investigative stories in particular, information is better presented in charts, graphs or maps than text.*

DEFENSE ATTORNEY: *A good editor defends reporters against angry sources, jealous colleagues, skittish newspaper executives, etc. Your reporters must believe you'll stand with them when the heat is on.*

PROSECUTING ATTORNEY: *Sometimes, you must play district attorney on the behalf of readers and put your reporters on the witness stand. After all, your primary responsibility — for your sake, your reporters' sake and your newspaper or station's sake — is to the readers and audiences. Sometimes, that means giving reporters the third degree (in a respectful manner, of course, and liberally using the pronoun "we"): How do we know this? Can we say this more clearly? Do we have statistics to support this conclusion? What's our best quote? What's our central point here, the one thing we don't want readers to miss? Is this fair? And so on.*

HUMORIST: *Keep it light. Yes, some stories can be matters of life and death. But even in those cases — in fact, especially in those cases — a well-timed wisecrack can ease the pressure and help maintain a good working environment.*

EVANGELIST: If you're an editor, you should be the Jerry Falwell of your newsroom, constantly spreading the gospel of good reporting up, down and across your organization. Most importantly, you should be helping your bosses understand why it's worth their while to invest the time and money good reporting requires. Find good stories done by other papers or stations, show them around and start discussions on how you can do similar — or better — work in your newsroom. And once your reporters are off for a month or two or six working on a big investigation, you must be their public-relations flak inside the newsroom, especially with other editors and reporters complaining about the amount of time your folks are getting.

BABYSITTER: Literally and figuratively. If your reporter's a dad or a mom who's up against a deadline and can't find childcare, offer to watch the kids. Similarly, do whatever you can to ease the stress of the conflicts of daily life for the people who work for you. In a figurative sense, you should babysit your reporters. Keep abreast of their daily activities, through daily conversations and a master electronic file. On long-term projects, have them give you a weekly synopsis or memo on the week's activities and developments.

CLERGY/CONFESSOR: Covet whatever or whomever you like. And if you pray to idols, that's your business. But there's one commandment you must follow: Thou shalt not lie. Never, ever deceive anyone in the newsroom; it will surely come back to haunt you. And always be especially straightforward with your reporters. Also, be someone to whom your reporters can confess their sins without fear of undue retribution or punishment. If they're unsure of a fact, concerned about a mistake, afraid of something, you want them to feel comfortable telling you.

HIT MAN: A great editor is not afraid to "pull the trigger," to be willing to publish a story that's likely to foment negative reaction and to take the heat when it comes down. There's another side of "pulling the trigger," also, one reporters don't talk much about but that's just as important: the willingness to cut your losses, to call it quits or to change direction on a story that just isn't panning out. If your reporters are doing meaningful, genuine reporting, it has to be OK for them to discover that there is no story, or that the story is different than you or they thought it was at the beginning of the process.

MIDWIFE: When a reporter's finally ready to give birth to a story, he or she needs a midwife to help with the delivery. That can mean anything from setting out a deadline schedule to buying him or her a burger and a beer in those tense hours just before publication. Most importantly, be there with and for the reporter.

RECRUITER: If you have the opportunity to recruit and hire, this is one of your most important roles. Don't sell it short. Build and maintain a network of quality journalists around the country and make that network work for you when you have an opening. The best thing any editor can do is to hire good people.

Discover Your Assets in the Newsroom

Now think again about the people and situations around you. Where can you find help in exercising your power?

First, look to your supporters. Cultivate them carefully and fairly. Too much attention to them and they become your pets, furthering division in the newsroom. Become dependent on their approval and you'll find them manipulating you. Keep your balance. The bigger tendency is to take them for granted while focusing on the problem-folk. Take stock of those co-operative souls, lend them an ear and regularly express appreciation.

The quiet leaders in your newsroom form another powerful group. Who are they? Susan Ager, columnist for the *Detroit Free*

Press, described them as the "soul of a newsroom. They go about their work, not calling much attention to themselves, but if they were gone it would make a big difference." These are the people who calm disturbances, who encourage the frustrated and enlist support by giving a word or two of advice. Often they are the newsroom veterans, but they don't have to have long tenure. In a sense they have referent power. Something about their personal qualities draws people to them. They are respected; they have influence. Turn to them. Bounce your ideas off them. They will help you think through your plans and, if they approve, provide an advance support network.

Don't forget the negative version of the quiet leaders. They stir discontent. They spread gossip, question decisions, see unfairness at every turn. They may not talk to you, but they are talking to everyone else. Challenge them. Encourage them to be a part of the solution rather than a part of the problem. If that fails, at least you can understand their discontent and address it.

Go to other critics. It takes a tough skin to hear them out, but you can learn from them, and often find ways to address their legitimate concerns.

The Humbling of an Editor

She swelled with pride when she became editor of a weekly newspaper within a year of finishing college. She had the title and the power. Then she learned what the power really offered. It meant, she said:

Writing all the stories when reporters let her down (she used her middle and maiden name for some bylines, her first and married name for others to make the staff look larger);

Coaxing the page designer to stay for one more issue when he became melancholy and threatened to quit;

Joking with the delivery guys on publication day so they wouldn't entertain themselves with funny cigarettes and fail to deliver the paper;

Setting type at 2 a.m. when equipment stalled and the real typesetter's husband demanded that she come home.

That experience wasn't fun, but it taught her something about the ambiguous power of editors. An editor must play many roles to get the job. But she can make a difference.

How would all this help a discouraged early morning caller? Maybe he will remember that his job is bigger than two problem reporters. Maybe he will renew himself by recalling how he had helped others and by looking for support from those around him. Maybe he could coax the older reporter into taking on the younger reporter as a project. Perhaps it is time for him to take a stand with a higher-up to find new ways of managing the two situations. Maybe it is a call to come out of the cave, and fight on.

CHAPTER FOUR
Support for Editors

Now that you have moved those few feet from your reporter's desk to an editor's desk, you are realizing that you have entered a new world. In this world, failure is often disguised until late.

Remember the quick response you may have received when you were a writer? "Good story, Sara; I liked your lead." "Um, Mike, why don't we identify the assailant?" It's unlikely you'll hear similar reactions to your new editing work. "Good job, Sara, I liked the way you asked for a lead and an outline from Mike, and the way you were able to be direct with him without being destructive." Not likely. As an editor, you can dig yourself into major difficulties before any one notices, much less offers a diagnosis and some help.

What's more, in many newsrooms, the things that are giving you and other editors the most trouble go unremarked, like a neurotic family that avoids talk about its difficulties. This kind of isolation is not universal, of course. You may have an alert supervisor who takes a systematic and constructive interest in you. But you cannot count on it.

In our experience with editors from a range of news operations — print, broadcast, online — the near-universal model for editor preparation boils down to sink or swim. So, just to be realistic, you should consider yourself the primary steward of your training and development. Who else is more interested?

There are newsrooms where the training of editors is taken seriously, although rarely before the new editors are already at work. The newsroom model, at best, is to put you behind the wheel and then, possibly, see about some training. Start from the assumption that you are in a job for which you are not fully prepared, and that no one, really, will notice until you start getting into difficulty.

So, what's next? How do you marshal the support that will help you succeed? Start with some analysis. In your first year or two you are going to absorb some core values and practices. You want to be careful what you learn, and from whom. Ask yourself what sort of newsroom do you work in. Recognize its strengths as well as its weaknesses. Is it a place where people are valued? How do editors talk about the people they supervise? Cynically? Is the language manipulative?

"Let's see," said the local news editor, "we need the story by five so we'll tell her we need it by four." There are far worse sins, but the editor is practicing a gamesmanship in which one product is the devaluation of truth. It is a solution to a problem — a writer who is chronically late — that creates its own problems.

Is your newsroom a place where the editors change reporters' work freely, treating it as the ore from which they will manufacture the product? In such a place, editors practice a form of secret editing. The reporters may dread looking at their stories as published, because they never know what they will find.

Maybe your newsroom is a place of such presumably democratic values that the editing is timid, and the editors fear the disapproval of the writers so much that the paper reeks of the indulgence of first-draft journalism. Oddly, we have seen some of the most sour editor-writer relations in newsrooms where the editors feared too much the disapproval of writers.

Perhaps your newsroom is a place where the editors have some confidence. In such an organization, a reasonable number of the writers will, if pressed, acknowledge that at least some of the editors know what they are doing and help writers improve their work.

Develop a sense of your newsroom's weaknesses and strengths, and the weaknesses and strengths of individual editors. Now you are ready to establish a support system for yourself. A support system has two purposes. First, to give you knowledge that will make you a better editor. Second, to encourage you when you need it.

To do this difficult work of being an editor, you need encouragement and help. There are three sources: editors in your newsroom, books you decide to acquire and become thoroughly familiar with, and friends and peers elsewhere. Use them all. None will hurt; most will help, if you allow them.

Find a Mentor

Do your best to find a mentor, or mentors. This trendy word has respectable origins. In the Odyssey, Mentor was entrusted with educating Telemachus, the son of Odysseus. Your mentor needs to be someone who seems to know what she is doing, and who is willing to take an interest in you.

Newspapers have experimented with mentoring "systems" with uncertain results, but with one reasonably clear conclusion:

A person who asks for help is more likely to benefit from it than a person who is offered the help. Someone swept into a mentoring system brought in like the latest corporate Hula-Hoop may resent the implication. What often seems to make a difference between success and failure in such systems is whether the newsroom considers itself a place where everyone keeps learning.

We are not, by the way, advising you to avoid mentoring systems, either as recipient or as creator, when you get the chance. But don't be passive. Don't wait for someone else to do the right thing for you. You do the right thing.

"This is not a finishing school," said the editor, whereupon everyone knew that the newspaper was not a learning organization and people were expected to pretend they knew it all. In newsrooms like this, people tend to keep their heads down, and that includes the editors. Training is thought of as something that remedies deficiencies, not something that helps good people get better. In such newsrooms, the unspoken goal of writers and editors is to be good enough to be ignored, because attention implies deficiency. You, on the other hand, are a new, or relatively new, editor. Your interest in having an experienced editor take a constructive interest in you ought to be an obvious good thing. So, ask for help. This will be easier if you have had the good fortune to land in a newsroom where questions are welcomed.

Find editors you think have something to teach you, and approach them. Ask good questions about your work, as though you were reporting a story. What am I doing well? What am I doing not so well? What are the three most important things about being an editor in this newsroom? When editors fail here, how does it happen? And on, and on.

As in reporting a story, don't swallow what you hear uncritically, but don't be quick to dismiss, either. Learn from colleagues. Some of the lessons may be negative; you may learn by example what not to do. But some will be positive. Good editors are to be found in most newsrooms, and you should identify them, and learn from them.

Acquire a Library

A good small library has psychological and practical value. Yes, you should have a good dictionary and be familiar with it. Add these books, and be familiar with them. Scan them often. Use them as reference works, use them to stimulate your thinking. On to the books.

First, *The Elements of Style* by William Strunk Jr. and E.B. White. This book's major value is as a call to respect the fundamentals of writing in English. Its supreme values, therefore, do not change. If anything, the most famous of its instructions, "Omit needless words," is more valuable than ever in these verbose days.

The Elements of Style was first published privately on the Cornell University campus in the early years of the 20th century. The author was William Strunk Jr. He used his so-called "little book" as a text in a course in correct English called English 8. One of his students in 1919 was E.B. White, who later became a well-known writer of essays and of books primarily for children (*Stuart Little, Charlotte's Web*).

In 1959, an American publisher brought out the book, with White's revisions. It has never been out of print since. It has been updated a bit here and there, but the main message – clarity, simplicity, concision – is unchanged. In 1988, Washington Post correspondent Blaine Harden won the coveted Best Newspaper Writing prize for best non-deadline writing. When he was asked who taught him to write, he replied that a college teacher had given him a copy of the Elements of Style and told him to memorize the book. He did.

The book contains an introduction and five short chapters, discussing rules of usage, principles of good composition, commonly misused expressions, some approaches to the holy grail, style. You may already know all the book has to teach you, but most people do not.

Second, *The Careful Writer* by Theodore M. Bernstein. Bernstein was the longtime arbiter of taste and usage at *The New York Times*. His book is now out of print, but can often be found in used book stores. It is an easy book to browse, and it will throw you a life preserver when you seem to be sinking yet again in a flood of hackneyed language. Consult it often; there is likely to be an entry for whatever is bothering you.

Third, *The Art and Craft of Feature Writing* by William Blundell. Blundell was a fine Wall Street Journal reporter. In the mid-80s, his paper asked him to teach other reporters how to report and write as well as he did. For a while, his teaching notes were bootlegged around the United States. Reporters liked his approach because he sympathized with their problems and yet knew their sins so well. The first section of the book is called "The disorganized, debilitated reporter." The last section in the final chapter is called "The anguish of young writers, and how some overcome it." Incidentally, Blundell, too, believes that the single best book is *The Elements of Style*. "If a writer were told he could read only one book about his craft, this would be the best choice. Its instruction in clarity, economy and grace is unequaled."

Fourth, *On Writing Well: An Informal Guide to Writing Nonfiction* by William Zinsser, a former *New York Herald-Tribune* writer and editor who has also taught writing. It is a sensible and optimistic book, and most struggling writers — to commit a redundancy — find it useful and encouraging. The chapter on simplicity is superb. Says Zinsser: "My purpose in *On Writing Well* is not to teach good nonfiction, or good journalism, but to teach good English that can be put to those uses, or to any uses. Don't assume that bad English can be good journalism, or good science writing, or good business writing. It can't. Good English is the only passport. To have a decent career in America you need to be able to write a succession of clear, decent sentences."

Fifth, *Coaching Writers: Editors and Reporters Working Together* by Roy Peter Clark and Don Fry. For years, Fry and Clark were the Batman and Robin of The Poynter Institute for Media Studies. In the Institute's formative years, they were principal influences in what you might now call the Poynter Way:

You will get better work done through cooperation than confrontation. Writing is not mysterious, at least not entirely. It can be understood, and that understanding can improve it. It takes the right vocabulary to be able to talk with writers usefully, and many editors lack that vocabulary. Paying attention to how people deal with each other in newsrooms can bring large gains.

In this book, Clark and Fry have codified all that they have learned. Hence the book takes you, the editor, through terrain ignored by most other books. There are a number of good books on writing. This is thus far the only book we know of on coaching.

Sixth, *The Effective Executive,* by Peter Drucker, which we mentioned in Chapter 1. This book is one of a kind. Peter Drucker did not actually invent management, although "father of management" is often used as a shorthand description of his role. He did study it, codify it and produce the language that describes it. He was born in Vienna in 1909 and eventually settled in California. He has seen more of life than most people, and if you check his list of publications you may just decide to go back to bed. His first big book, *The Concept of the Corporation*, was on General Motors. Much of whatever you have absorbed about who managers are and what they do likely originated with this book, for this book created the idea of management as a set of beliefs and skills. In *The Effective Executive*, Drucker does for management and, yes, leadership, what Strunk and White do for writing good English. He reduces, as much as possible, a sprawling tangle of practices to a handful of principles. His book came out in 1966, and has never been out of print. It consists of seven chapters, concisely titled: Effectiveness Can Be Learned; Know Thy Time; What Can I Contribute; Making Strength Productive; First Things First; The Elements of Decision-Making; Effective Decisions; Conclusion: Effectiveness Must be Learned. That conclusion may be the biggest contribution to your mental health. If you accept it, you will not be surprised to find yourself making mistakes. You will see the problem as how to gain knowledge and skill in handling people, not as how to find some mysterious "natural leader" within.

Find Peers

Isolation is the secret disease of editing. Writers in organization have the implied brother and sisterhood of numbers of people in similar circumstances. This tends to play out in an us-versus-them loyalty in which the unspoken compact is this: "You praise my stuff and I'll praise yours and we'll all scoff at the editors."

Editors have no such compact, although they have been known to do a little grousing among themselves. Make friends of your peers. You need pals who share your kind of life and who understand what it takes to actually get a piece of good writing into print.

Section III
Craft Skills for the Long Run

CHAPTER FIVE
An Editor's Language

Shoppers at a mall found the bodies of three children shortly after parents reported the siblings missing. Live coverage of the story interrupted programming throughout the day. In the evening, news anchors cut in to say police were about to make a statement. We go to the scene with reporter Jason Jay.

"We're waiting here where police will make a statement any minute now," Jason says.

"What's the scene like?" asks anchor Jim Smith.

"Well we have been gathered here most of the afternoon, and now we're awaiting the announcement. Police Chief Wade Moss should address us momentarily."

Nothing happens.

"Jason, while we wait, would you review the events of the day?"

The reporter retells the story. He ends by saying, "We're told Chief Moss will appear any minute through this door."

A camera shot zooms in tight on a screened door. Nothing happens. Inside, a man goes about his work.

Silence, then reporter and anchor talk simultaneously.

"Maybe we should mention that..."

"...Jason, let's discuss..."

After a moment of talking over each other, the conversation moves to the criminal record of the father. Reporter Jay gives a long account of the father's past.

He finishes and there's silence. The split screen shows the reporter at the scene and two anchors behind a desk, all looking surprised. Finally one anchor says, "Sorry, Jason, I was listening to the producer."

Cut to commercial.

Sometimes things fall apart. The live shot take an unexpected turn, or no turn. The juicy feature vaporizes. Daily stories turn out to be, in one editor's phrase, "about as exciting as a pail of spit." You can scream, lecture, or brush up the old resume, but those steps won't change the outcome.

This section offers weapons to battle story meltdown. Stories, good or bad, don't just happen. The myth says when things work well, the story tells itself. When they don't, we believe we're prisoners to story block. When the unexpected happens, we're programmed simply to react. Most newsrooms get by day to day, feeding the beast, churning out story after story. Excellence rarely emerges from "getting by."

There is a better way to do journalism. Good stories derive from three practices:

Using careful front-end work;
Understanding the writing process;
Employing systematic follow-up.

Like many things, easier said than done.

You must lead your staff in understanding, accepting, and

applying the practices. Mysterious grunts won't do it. You need a language, a vocabulary, to talk about stories more precisely than newsrooms typically do.

You need a language to talk about story diagnosis, about news coverage goals, about the communities you want to serve, and about how far you will go to get a story.

If the stories are going to get better, your staff will have to improve; and if they are to move forward, you will have to lead.

Front-end Work: Getting Ahead of the Story

Years ago a sociologist studied how reporters learn the policies, habits and sacred cows of a newsroom. His report, "Social Control in the Newsroom,"[5] noted primary ways that staffers learn what's expected of them. They learn from:

What's not allowed in a story;
How stories are played;
Reprimands and negative non-verbal signals of bosses;
The interests and affiliations of the organization's leaders;
Gossip.

The study also noted that reporters tend to bypass policy when norms aren't clear, when they know far more about the story than editors, and when they have star status.

You probably know all that, but the study is an important reminder. Little things in a newsroom carry big messages. What

---

[5] Warren Breed, "Social Control in the News Room," in *Mass Communication* by Wilber Schramm, 1960.

are your staffers learning? How do you use words, policies, and actions to improve your news report?

Let's start with your standards. The first section of this book focused on your mission. We asked you to be clear about the things that you stand for. Now it's time for you to examine your vision for your newsroom. Try answering the following questions. If you are really clear about the answers, you should be able to answer in 10 words or fewer.

What Does Your News Department Stand For?

Do you have a branding or company slogans, such as "All the news that's fit to print," "We're on your side," "News leader for ..." Does the slogan mean anything? Does it inspire and guide the staff? What is your message to the staff? Can you state a compelling news mission that is in line with company goals? If not, what is the difficulty, and how do you overcome it? In short, what is the message that you want in the heads of staffers as they go about their work?

Whom Do You Serve?

That's easy, you say. We serve the people of this city. Really? Look at a week of your reports. Who's there and who's not? How well do you represent various segments of the population? If you downplayed or skipped covering the death of a major teen music idol, you might not be hearing the voices of young people in your area. If you cover certain low-income residents as only criminals or victims, you might not know the inspiring stories of daily life in their world. If you aren't comfortable showing religion in daily life, you might miss the things that people think about and act on. So whom are you serving? Are you limited to the interests of people in your newsroom or of senior management? Think about how your perception of news is affected by how you define your area of service.

What Do Your Staff Members Expect of Each Other?

Have you ever talked about this? You assume there's a mutual expectation to work hard, behave professionally and ethically, and go the extra mile to get the story. Consider how those goals mean different things to different people. Does working hard mean regularly putting in long hours? What happens when getting the story raises ethical questions? Do staff members know what to do? What do your policies and practices tell them?

What are Your Goals for the News Report?

Journalists usually say news should be accurate, complete, balanced, fair, etc. That response focuses on news qualities. A different response might focus on audience; news should be understandable to a broad range of the community, or compelling to various levels of society. The business response might call for a report that draws a desired market share of consumers. Or is your goal a report that wins awards? There are all kind of responses. The question is, what do you expect of your news report? How would your staff answer this question?

How Have You Planned for Big Stories?

The first four questions dealt with getting heads together. This one is about the tactics of preparation. You never know what news might break, but you can be ready.

A gasoline explosion in Bellingham, Wash. left Dean Kahn of *The Bellingham Herald* reflecting on planning. Here's an edited version of an e-mail, reflecting a staff survey, that he sent to training editors:

When a gasoline pipeline ruptured and ignited, three were killed — two 10-year-old boys playing in a park and an 18-year-old man fly-fishing in the same park. Flames reached 100 feet high, stopping just short of the freeway and downtown, and smoke rose 30,000 feet.

The explosion became fodder for congressional debate over pipeline safety. More than that, it truly shook the community and challenged the newsroom of The Herald, *a 27,000 daily circulation paper.*

The pipeline exploded at 5 p.m. on a Thursday, as reporters were wrapping up their day. Several senior editors were out of town.

What follows are some lessons learned from the experience. Some are familiar. Some are new, at least to me. I hope the list, in some way, helps you prepare for whatever disaster might befall your community.

Decide early which reporter will write the initial main bar. We picked a veteran who's a quick, graceful writer and who had handled such an assignment before. It made the first coverage immeasurably better.

Something we didn't do quickly enough was to assign a reporter or librarian to search the Internet for info about the pipeline company and the government agencies involved. Once we got a reporter on the task, we ended up with a good story about how the federal pipeline agency has been criticized for a lax attitude toward safety.

Think ahead about news features for the coming days. One reporter decided early to focus on firefighters' initial response and came away with a colorful story full of heroics.

Be prepared to handle a flood of citizen photographs, some on film, many via Internet. Your editors should be clear about how to handle such submissions and decide early about pay, follow-up usage, AP usage, and other photo issues.

We asked the public to send us accounts of where they were and what they did when the pipeline exploded. We ended up with a huge volume of letters and photos, which we ran about a week after the explosion. Such disasters linger long in a community's collective memory, especially in a small town. Readers appreciate contributing to that history with their own recollections.

It took longer than expected to get a county map showing pipelines routes. Don't wait for a disaster; get local maps of pipelines and other industrial and utility facilities before they cause trouble.

As reporters went out the door, we told each of them to focus on "people and details, details, details." Certain details stood out and brought tears.

Something else we didn't do, but should have, was to develop a file of basic information: times, job titles, unusual spellings, etc., that would be needed as the days progressed and as more of the explosion's details became boilerplate in later stories.

From the start, develop a running list of contacts, phone numbers, sources, etc.

Early on, develop a planning budget for short- and long-term follow-up stories, then hold regular meetings with your reporters who are pursuing the stories.

Be bold on all fronts. The Herald did not hire an aircraft the day of the explosion, so we were forced to use other people's aerial photos of the mushroom cloud, towering flames and, on following days, the burned scar through the park.

You might consider having a stash of point-and-shoot or disposable cameras for reporters to use when a major story breaks.

Radio phones and regular phones worked after the explosion, but not cell phones. More cell-radio combination phones would have been helpful.

The people who run the emergency-response agency in your city or county discuss what they do when disasters occur. Learn their procedures and paperwork routines, before a disaster hits.

Being prepared can mean a basic drill that all editors know:[6]

Main: what happened (with map and chronology)
Victims: a wrap-up?
Profiles: break-outs of victims?
Record of plane, bus, train etc. with graphic
Investigation: what went wrong, what's next?
Impact: on industry, transportation, town, whatever?
Heroes?
Emergency response?
Medical aspect?
Scenes: at the site, at the airport, at the whatever?
Other incidents like this (graphic)
Lists of injured, dead, wounded, whatever?
Broadcast performance

Front-end work, then, focuses on preparing your staffers to do their best work by giving them a picture of what they stand for, what's expected of them and a model for thinking ahead. These five questions are a guide. Consider what questions would be most effective in your newsroom.

---

[6] From the late Dee Murphy of the *Newark Star-Ledger.*

John Lansing, who has served as a television news executive in Chicago, Minneapolis, Detroit, and Cleveland, uses four questions on principles:

What are the principles that you believe in and that define your work?

What are the principles that drive your newsroom?

What principles are shared?

What principles do you want to bring to the larger organization? To the newsroom?

Lansing said you needn't come up with answers to the questions alone. You don't want to lead by a speech but through conversations with various segments of the staff, then maybe a full-group exchange. They need to have a voice in the principles that they will be expected to practice.

Here's one reminder before we leave the topic of front-end work. All your effort is in vain if you don't follow up by practicing the principles. You have to make deadline decisions that are in line with goals you've led in articulating. You have to hold others accountable for the same. You'll need to acknowledge endeavors in line with the goals, and challenge actions that depart from them.

Your voice should be a reminder in each staffer's head about how to cover the news, but your actions will speak much louder than anything you say.

The Writing Process

We could claim that the Writing Process is a sophisticated method designed to help journalists to produce better stories, but enter some fifth-grade classrooms and you'll see youngsters busily following the process: getting ideas, reporting, organizing, drafting and editing. The Writing Process has range, like the man closely associated with its development. Donald Murray won the Pulitzer Prize for editorial writing at the Boston Herald in 1954. He worked as a writing coach at the *Boston Globe, Providence Journal* and other newspapers, chaired the Department of English at the University of New Hampshire, authored more than a dozen books on writing, and 45 years after winning the Pulitzer, writes a column for the *Boston Globe.*

Much of his work has consisted of showing writers how to get the words out, to get them down quickly to stay ahead of the internal censor,[7] to let the words speak about what the writer is trying to say, and then to polish the piece. The process helps, not only in finishing a story, but also in tracking a writer's strengths and weaknesses, so that the writer can improve.

Here are the five steps of the Writing Process:

The Idea

Several years ago a pop singer had a hit with a song called *Making Love Out of Nothing at All.* Many a storyteller labors over work that falls short because the idea is really nothing at all. It looked good initially, but somewhere along the way it faded. Good stories need a good start. Writers have to focus on story ideas. Where do you and the staff get good story ideas?

Here's the start of a checklist:

Observations: What do you see around you? Consider the commute to work. Most people take the same route each day and

---

[7] Donald M. Murray, *Write to Learn,* Harcourt Brace Jovanovich College Publisher, 1993, pg. 1.

the view becomes stale. Lead your newsroom in taking a different route one week out of every month. Get off the highways and drive through neighborhoods. Take mass transit. Look around at the people. Think about the things they see and do everyday. Question changes, things that don't work, or things that work well. Seek out the stories that affect the community or segments of it.

Government: In the great rush to cover people, not meetings, the news media lost something. Indicators suggest a decline in covering government. The real action is with the people, but stories start in meetings, legislative acts, and government reports. Look there for ideas, then add flesh to stories by covering the people affected.

Business and non-profits: This is similar to government coverage. Many newsrooms assign someone to cover business, but few cover non-profits, which are a major portion of the economy. Non-profits include large foundations and institutes, and small service organizations. Periodically they yield a big story, usually on misuse of funds. They should be a part of regular coverage showing their impact, good work, challenges, and misdeeds.

People in stories: Every completed interview should lead to an idea for another story, often on a totally unrelated topic.

Rolodex: Who has the best collection of names and numbers on your staff? A good collection is organized and up to date. It should be diverse: public officials, public figures, and common folks; people of various colors, and ethnic and racial groups; representatives of educational, recreational, religious, medical and interest groups; lower-level contacts at government and social agencies, such as receptionists who have first contact with clients, and former sources. Make a call each day, or set aside some time each week for calls to draw fresh ideas.

The walking Rolodex: Same as above, but on foot rather than by phone. Writers prize editors who help them build in time to make these contacts.

Targeting a community: A meeting of editors included a trip to a community center. The center director spoke briefly to the group, then sent the editors out to find story ideas in the building. They were amazed at the ideas that sprang from the bulletin board, conversations with center employees, and observations of activities. One said, "Why can't we do this at home?" Assign staffers to a different community one or two days a week and see what the visits generate. Yes, that means pulling someone off a daily story. The rewards will be worth it.

Reports: Buried in dull-looking reports lie fascinating statistics on society. Match them with similar reports from a year, five years, 10 years earlier and you have pictures of change, sometimes in surprising directions. Draw in staffers throughout your newsroom to help on this. Every find won't lead to a full story. Some will lead to a brief or a regular listing of data. These short treatments can be as powerful, or more so, than a full story.

Online: The world awaits on the web. Ideas include in-depth information on stories you're covering; unusual people, topics or information; tabulations of where people are going on the web; and the growth and changes of the web itself, as well as stories on what it offers.

The swipe file: What better way to show your appreciation of a well-done story from elsewhere than to steal the idea. Read, watch, and listen to news presentations to find the ideas that will inspire you.

Daily life: Challenge your staff to come up with one budget item a week from their lives. It could be a story on a medical condition or problems with child care. Great stories might begin with commuting problems or car purchases. The key is to get beyond the personal to find the broader community issue. If staffers can't come up with good stories, encourage them to get a life.

These are a few ideas for starters. Let your staff brainstorm others. Encourage them to come up with their own ideas, and always have a few fresh ones to hand out. Accept that your brilliant ideas won't always be appreciated. Many of them will lead to good stories, some will inspire writers to work harder at generating their own ideas, and a few will be left for you to do, proving that you can still write as well as edit.

The keys in this first step of the writing process are to generate a good list of idea sources and regularly work the list. Find an idea, then narrow the focus. What part of the story does the writer expect to tell? Get it down to something manageable, leave room for change in case reality intrudes on the expected, and you're off.

Reporting

Here's where most reporters feel comfortable. They know how to get out and get the story. You can help by challenging them to get past the most frequently heard sources to include more voices in their reporting. Encourage them to think about: Who's affected? Who's been through a similar experience, and what did they learn? Who has an unusual perspective? Motivate them with information that you've found from new sources, such as the Internet. Nora Paul lists ways online information helps in reporting:[8]

> To locate people as primary sources;
> To find documents and secondary sources;
> To locate specific facts, statistics, ready-reference information;
> To get up to speed on a topic;
> To stay current on a beat.

Within the limitations of time, and available information, the reporter's goal is to find the facts and opinions that answer the most important questions. Often those come from official sources. So be it. Let's be grateful for them but understand their limitations. They usually tell the facts but little about the human effect. To tell the feelings, reporters turn to people involved. They might add facts, and they tell of experiences, hopes, defeats and victories.

Good storytelling also calls on the writer to present images and set the scene.

Gene Roberts, former editor of the *Philadelphia Inquirer* and managing editor of *The New York Times*, made the point to Columbia University graduates:[9]

> *My first newspaper job was with the* Goldsboro News-Argus, *which, to the under-informed, is the leading newspaper in Wayne*

---

[8] Nora Paul, *Computer Assisted Research: A guide to tapping online information for journalists*, The Poynter Institute and Bonus Books, 1999. pgs. 8-10.
[9] "From Rural Ramblin' to a Bunker in Hue," Publisher's Note by Joan Konner, *Columbia Journalism Review*, September/October 1996.

County, North Carolina. The editor of the paper was Henry Belk. He was then in his 60s, and he was blind — he was sightless. This was in the 1950s. But he wore battered fedora hats like newsmen wore in the movies in the 1930s and '40s, when he could still see. He was tall — no, towering. There were no ready-made canes to fit his 6-foot 7-inch form, so he tapped with a stretched cane made especially for him out of aluminum. He cared passionately about the paper. And it was read to him, word for word, over the years by a succession of high-school students. And in the mornings, his wife, Lucille, once a journalist herself, read him the newspaper published in the state capital, The Raleigh News and Observer.

He was awesomely informed. Most days at the office, he would call out from his cubicle, and say such things as, "On page 17 of the News and Observer, in column three, halfway down the fold, there is a three-inch story about Goldsboro, under an 18-point head." Then he would demand, "Why didn't we have it?" Mr. Belk was nothing if not demanding. Often when he heard my footfall in the morning, he would summon me to his cubicle and criticize the "Ramblin' in Rural Wayne" column I had written the day before. On too many days, alas, my writing was insufficiently descriptive. "You aren't making me see," Mr. Belk would say. "Make me see."

In an effort to force me to be graphic and vivid, he made me end every column with a paragraph labeled, "Today's Prettiest Sight." Let me tell you, it's tough to go into a poolroom in your hometown for an end-of-the-work-day beer known as the guy who writes "Today's Prettiest Sight." But I persevered. It took me years to appreciate it, but there is no better admonition to the writer than "make me see." There is no truer blueprint for successful writing than making your reader see. It is the essence of great writing and great reporting.

People still cry out for news reports that help them see what's going on. We do that with compelling graphics and photojournalism. That comes from early and frequent collaboration between the "word" staff and the "picture" staff. It comes from good descriptions of scenes, gestures, and other actions. It comes also as reporters appeal to all the senses by using their own five senses in the reporting.

By the time writers present the facts and opinions, feelings and images, the meaning might be clear. The storyteller must make sure she has done all she can to explain the effects of events. Often we're not sure what the story means. We must let the community know as much as we can, as clearly as we can.

The reporting stage is the time to gather all the information, all the details that best tell the story. Remind reporters to report widely and write narrowly. They must cast a wide and purposeful net, with an eye on story focus. Then they are ready for an important step before they write or produce.

Organizing

The unorganized story is confusing. No matter how thorough the reporting, how engaging the visuals, or how well-crafted the writing, the story falls short because readers must struggle to understand it.

This step requires writers to think through what they want to say before they begin composing. They need to map the story by writing the answers to two questions:

What is this story about?

and

What's the best way for me to tell it?

The first question is about theme, the second is about form.

Most writers begin a piece by asking themselves, "What's my lead or intro?" This process says you begin instead by asking the point of the story. The point is not:

City Council met today.

It might be:

City Council voted to raise water rates.

Or maybe:

Water rates will increase by 25 percent.

Or even:

Water rates will be the nation's highest.

The goal is not to write a lead or even a sentence. It is to write a focus statement. Ask, "With all this good information, what story should we tell?" Now's the time to make final shifts from the original idea, and to narrow the story rather than trying to tell too much. Some say you should be able to express the statement in six words or fewer. That's a test to see if you've settled on a tight, clear idea. Some suggest the "tell it to Mom" approach. Imagine yourself calling a loved one and telling the highlight of your story in one sentence. That's a test of whether your focus is compelling.

Collect other methods for forming and testing the story focus, but be sure your writers think about the point before they start writing. This is the key for moving from well-reported stories that disappoint to good writing.

After you've settled on a point, decide what elements best support it. What's the first point to support your focus statement, and what goes after that? What's the best order to present each element. How will the story end? Your story map will allow you to start writing and continue to the end without a lot of doubling back and making false starts that lead to tangents. On paper your map should look like a casual outline with six or so words or phrases.

Story shapes: Consider one other organizing step before you're ready to write. The last step is thinking about the story's shape. How will you tell the story? Here are a few choices:

Chronological: This is the most natural telling. You start at the beginning and go to the end, using time as the organizing principle. That works for shorter stories and longer pieces that have strong beginnings, middles, and ends.

Inverted pyramid: This unnatural form has a history back to the Civil War. It worked well then when telegraph lines were likely to falter at any time. This form made sure the most important points got through since they were at the top.

Some endorse it now in the belief that a hurried society prefers the good stuff followed by a descending order of lesser stuff. Maybe. Writing coach Don Fry points out that the form teaches readers that the longer you stay with the story the worse it will get.

Suspended interest: This one reverses the inverted pyramid by holding the main point until the end. This works well in telling jokes. It pops up as a useful form in some briefs. Beyond that, writers use it successfully, but it takes an interesting topic and strong writing to hold an audience to the end.

Fry and Roy Peter Clark, senior scholar at The Poynter Institute, used shapes to characterize the organization of some stories:

Hourglass: This begins like the inverted pyramid by moving from the most important point to lesser elements, but then it starts over with a chronological retelling that adds many new facts and details. Here's a version of it:

The two games in East High's match with Northside took on two completely different looks last night. But fortunately for the Bears, the results were the same.

East trailed big in the first game, rallied, but lost 16-14. The Bears then jumped out to a big lead in the second game. But Northside stormed back and took the match with a 17-15 victory.

Two different beginnings, nearly identical endings. For Bears coach Paul Morris, it summed up his team's season.

"It was the same that I've seen happen all year long," Morris said. "A slow start, then we come back, but it's not quite enough to win the game. Then in Game 2, we come out on a tear, stall around 10; they come back and then victory squirts away in the end."

And that was what happened yesterday.

The Northside Knights, 20-2 and ranked fourth in Class 3A, jumped to a 9-1 lead behind the strong serving of Loni Weathers, who recorded five of her team's nine points.

Notice the story is an inverted pyramid through Coach Morris' quote. It could end there and you'd have the main facts. Instead a transition follows and a retelling begins with greater detail. This form is useful in police reports and other action stories. It allows the writer to tell the big picture quickly for readers who scan, and yet provide the details for those who want to read on. The form can be adopted for longer, in-depth reports.

Stacked Blocks: This works very well in long stories with a lot of sources. It allows the writer to tell the story by bringing one or two characters on stage at a time, letting them say and do what they need, then allowing them to exit before bringing on the next characters or ideas. The design is to tell one segment of the story, then move to the next, largely self-contained segment. The style promotes clarity when there's a lot going on. In long stories it allows readers to take a break and come back to the story.

Q: The story starts at a dramatic point, flashes back to events that led up to that point, returns to the dramatic point and ends. An example is a story that begins during a trial, flashes back to events that led to the trial, returns to the trial, maybe just prior to the verdict, adds that scene and ends.

You get the point. It's not about geometry or a debate of preferred forms. It is a suggestion that there are many ways to tell a story, but writers need to make a decision before they begin to write. Encourage them to think about the shapes of stories they read and see, and to organize their stories before the telling.

Drafting

This step is quick. If you carry out the first three steps well, this one is simply a matter of following your story map as you write or produce. Many journalists find they are better off not looking in their notebooks at this point. That helps them focus on the most vivid points of their reporting. They can go back to make sure details are correct. Right now they are letting the story flow in line with the organizational plan.

The most difficult element here is not going back to correct, rewrite, and polish. The lead's not great. No problem. Just keep writing. If writers really don't have the discipline to keep writing, Fry encourages them to turn off the computer screen. That will force them to move forward because they can't see to go back and make changes. It looks strange to passers-by but works well until the phone rings and they forget where they were in the writing.

The other problem with drafting is ensuring that the writer

plan her time so she can edit. If she doesn't have time, drafting is a failure. There's the temptation to turn in the draft and let someone else clean it up. Wrong. Nobody knows the story like the writer. No one is responsible for a well-edited piece but the writer.

Editing

The final step for the writer is to go back and clean up the rough edges. Al Tompkins suggested some steps for "Clearer, Stronger Writing" (next page). Here are some checkpoints:

Facts: Make sure that what you've written is what happened;

Spelling: Check and recheck names, titles, words with unusual spellings, your most frequently misspelled words, and everything else. Use a spell check but keep training your eye;

Numbers: Recheck the digits, especially phone numbers. Check other numbers, make sure all math is correct, give thought to whether numbers (crowd estimates, salaries, etc.) seem logical;

Grammar: Subjects and verbs must agree; pronouns need correct antecedents; modifiers must not dangle; make your English teacher proud;

Style: When it comes to repairing your story, leave the copy desk feeling like the washing machine repair guy who has nothing to do.

Before you finish:

Eliminate unnecessary words, phrases, and sections. Concise writing improves the pace and overall flow. Reread to make sure surrounding grammar and syntax are correct.

Use "gold coins." Look for story sag and place good quotes, anecdotes, or telling details there to boost the piece.

Check legal matters. Make sure you're covered in everything you say. Raise the flag if you spot concerns;

CLEARER, STRONGER WRITING
By Al Tompkins
The Poynter Institute

1. Tell the story in three words or OTPS, one theme per story, one thought per sentence. Select, don't compress, what goes in your stories. The stuff that does not make it into the story will make great tags, follow-ups, or additional material for Internet sites.

2. Tell complex stories through strong characters. Readers and viewers will remember what they feel longer than what they know. Characters help me understand how the complex facts you uncovered affect people.

3. Objective copy, subjective sound. Let the characters evoke emotions, express feelings, and opinions in their soundbites. The journalists' copy should contain objective words, facts, and truths.

4. Use active verbs, not passive. Consider the difference between "the gun was found" and "the boy found the gun." Ask "Who did what?" and you will write stronger and more informed stories.

5. No subjective adjectives. Your lawyer and your viewers will thank you. No more "fantastic-unbelievable-gut wrenching" or "mother's worst nightmare."

6. Give viewers a sense for the passage of time in your story. Make me feel you have spent some time by showing me the character in more than one setting, in more than one situation.

7. Remember, leads tell me "so what," stories tell me "what" and tags tell me "what's next."

Be sure you've made ethically sound choices. Big picture matters should have been addressed early. At this point make sure you haven't included information that's high on the interest scale but low on showing good judgment;

Give an ear to story flow. Read it out loud. Adjust sentence lengths and phrasing to improve the pace.

The Writing Process serves several purposes. For writers, it is a wedge against writer's block. When the ideas and words won't come, they aren't left with frustration and the snack machines. Instead, they can figure out where they are in the process and think about what's missing. If there's a gap, the answer is usually found in the previous step. Can't determine what the story is about? Go back to the reporting and see what's missing. Having trouble drafting? Look back to the organization and see if the story plan is solid. The process helps writers and editors figure out what's going on with the story and what needs to be done next.

It also improves the language for talking about stories. It helps you identify parts of a story and talk about elements that are working or need work. Concrete terms help writers much more than pained body language or an eruption of invectives. Allow the process to lead the way to more precise story talk. Create your own terms, and make them clear and helpful. Once a newsroom starts talking about stories, it is primed to learn a lot from examining other news stories and other forms of stories.

Finally, the process helps you work with writers on their overall strengths and weaknesses. Some writers need to improve their ability to focus a story. They try to cover too much with no clear idea of what story they are to write. Some seem to be poor spellers or lack basic language skills, when the real problem is that they aren't leaving time to edit their work. Help them pace themselves. Some journalists love to report but dislike writing. They need to discipline themselves to know when to stop reporting and give more time to their writing or producing. The writing process will help you diagnose their problems.

After the Story

If a tree falls in the forest and no one hears it, will it make any noise?

If a reporter produces a story and no one says anything, has the reporter's work been in vain? We've looked at the front-end work required in a newsroom and at the writing process. The last step is a look at what happens after the stories go public. It is at this point that newsrooms show themselves to be part of a communications industry that does not communicate very well. As editor you must be prepared for two responses to stories: the external and the internal. The most likely external responses are usually in this order: public complaint, followed by public quiet, then public appreciation. When complaints come, you have the challenge of respecting and addressing the unhappy parties, while supporting your staff. When staff members are wrong, you need to be firm, but in as private a manner as feasible. You serve the public by letting them know you heard their concerns, you are acting on those concerns, if appropriate, and by letting readers and viewers in on the news gathering process, including where it might have broken down. Failures in the process ought to point at the newsroom and policies, not at individuals. Ignoring angry calls is not the answer.

When the public expresses appreciation, join in the celebration. Look for ways to highlight calls, letters to the editors, certificates or awards that commend staff work. Seek your own methods of honoring above-average performance. Make rewards consistent.

You rise in staff esteem when you fill that typical void of silence. You are your reporters' first audience. They bring stories to you that you edit and assist in moving to production. You will often be their last audience, too. If no one from the public or newsroom comments on a piece, you ought to do so. That lets a writer know someone saw the work. It is an opportunity to have a few words on weaknesses in the piece and a few words on what works.

Most writers feel starved for feedback; feed them.

Each day you will try to cram 14 hours of work into an eight-plus hour day, but find time to let your staffers know their work was not in vain.

The editor's language has great bearing on the craft in your newsroom. You will set the tone in how staff think about their work, understand the stories that they produce and in the way that they grow. Your language will occasionally be expressed in speeches. Staffers will hear it more clearly in the way you lead them in defining group goals, and in the way you act. When you hit it right, they will hear your voice in their heads guiding them to do their best work.

ADVICE TO A JOURNALIST

The late Dee Murphy, an editor at the Newark Star-Ledger, *wrote this classic note to a bureau reporter:*

Be diligent about the basics: Report to work on time. Make the police and court checks. File beat notes each week with new story ideas.

Read the *Star-Ledger* and *Asbury Park Press* daily. Educate yourself in the issues and topics in the news in other shore areas. The library can assist you in this.

Be prepared each day to discuss with the metro editors the news, topics in the news, and issues that are developing in which your beat plays a role. Know what's going on.

Develop the sources within the communities and county — officials, law enforcement, professionals, business people, community groups — to be knowledgeable about issues and topics worthy of coverage.

Develop story ideas for your beat that have the potential for Page One and Jersey Page display. When you and your editors have agreed to pursue a story, produce it in a timely manner.

Produce stories daily and a Sunday take-out at least once a month.

Produce stories that are well-researched, well-organized, and contain the necessary elements — interviews, background, statistical data, context — to be published.

CHAPTER SIX
The Teaching Editor

Educators asked a television news executive to name the best universities for producing TV journalists. Faces passed through his mind and so did schools. It didn't take him long to decide that high on his list was "Carole Kneeland University." Kneeland, former news director at KVUE-TV, Austin, Texas, didn't lead a journalism school, she led a newsroom. But in that newsroom she was a great teacher.

A month before her death she wrote about her system for operating a learning newsroom. She encouraged learning by:

Including staff members in the hiring and training of co-workers;

Offering formal training sessions in-house with the goal of having at least one opportunity for each person each quarter;

Providing additional training for each person away from the station once each year;

Expecting staff to teach what they learned upon their return from a training trip;

Allowing staff to make decisions about their work and encouraging them to take risks.

She also taught through her coaching and by her example as a journalist and newsroom leader.

A learning environment energizes a newsroom. More attention turns to improving news coverage, and less to gossip and complaints. Company-paid time away to learn becomes a valued reward for good work. The heart of a learning environment, however, is the editor. You create opportunities for learning. You also have to teach.

We've suggested ways of shaping the newsroom culture and of looking at writing as a process. This chapter focuses on what you could teach. We'll look at "Levels of Storytelling" from the minimum acceptable report to compelling stories. You might also teach about qualities of good writing found in award-winning stories, and why good stories fall short of greatness. Finally, we look at how you, as editor, can keep growing in your craft.

Levels of Storytelling

In Chapter 4 we told of an editor who struggled with reporters on opposite ends of the career ladder. A young reporter needed to master the basic story, while the senior writer needed rejuvenation. How do you teach folks with very different abilities and in various stages of growth? How do you set standards that encompass a minimum level for rookies and yet challenge veterans to keep improving? Journalism educators Mel Mencher and Stuart

Adam separately developed three-tiered rankings of news stories.[10] Consider this variation as a hierarchy for continued growth in your staff's stories.

Level I — The Clean Report

What's your minimum acceptable standard for a story? How about this: The story should be clear and free of basic errors. The facts give a report that makes sense. It is accurate. The mechanics (spelling, grammar, style) are sound, and it doesn't raise questions that aren't answered or present legal or ethical problems. Think of it this way. If all the stories in your report were clean, you might not dazzle or surprise, but you would inform. Your measure of service would be that people could understand the story and not have questions.

Here's an example:

---

[10] In *News Reporting and Writing* (fourth ed., Wm. C. Brown Publishers, 1987, p. 237) Melvin Mencher wrote of three layers of reporting. Writing on: (1) source-originated material such as speeches, (2) spontaneous events requiring the reporter's observations and enterprise, and (3) interpretation and explanation that looks at causes and consequences.

G. Stuart Adam, who wrote *Notes Toward a Definition of Journalism*, presents three levels: Reporting I is hard news requiring fact gathering and mastery of the foundations of reporting; Reporting II adds news judgement and the skills for writing long narratives and documentaries, improving the skills of narrative writing; Reporting III includes specialized reporting, investigative pieces, analyses, and criticism requiring the skills of a critic.

SOUTHWEST CLUB SCHEDULES MEETING TO FIGHT PARKWAY

The Southwest Club has battled against the Heritage Parkway for years. That fight will continue Thursday, as the club holds a town hall meeting designed to inform residents and spur action.

"Come learn about the Heritage Road," a club advertisement reads, "and how much it's really going to cost you!"

The meeting will be at the City Armory, First Street at U.S. 40, Clarkville. Doors will open at 6 p.m.

The parkway's first phase, which will end at Myers Road, already is being built. Next month the state will announce plans to build the second phase.

Supporters say the parkway will provide a scenic route around the city, but the club says it will invite urban sprawl.

Checklist for Level I — The Clean Report

Accurate: Facts and meaning, names and numbers are correct. It might help to have beginning writers highlight every fact, assertion, name, and number to indicate they have verified each one.

Clear: An average person can understand it in one pass.

Informative: The story tells all that's reasonable for this version about the who, what, when, where, why, and how.

Fair: An effort is made to represent all sides. Ask about stakeholders and how they are represented in, and affected by, the story.

Grounded: Subjects match verbs; pronouns match antecedents; sentences, punctuation, spelling, and style all pass muster.

Focused: The writer and audience agree on the point of the story.

Worthwhile: The story has impact on the community. The public is rewarded by time spent with this story.

That's a plateful, but there's one more teaching point, and it is a big one:

Values: We assume that a person who can punctuate a sentence knows journalists neither buy news nor take gifts from sources. Many won't understand journalistic ethics unless you teach them. Use a Code of Conduct if that works for you or simply state and restate what you stand for. In addition, teach an ethical process that guides your people in working through thorny problems. Most of all, on deadline practice what you teach.

Teach the importance of diversity. Folks in your community come in various shades and with different backgrounds and beliefs. Your job is to serve all of them. Teach staffers how to find stories that address the needs of different segments of the community and to find a range of voices for stories. Practice what you teach by making sure your community is represented in the makeup of your staff.

Teach a love for the community. Journalists have the obligation and the privilege of representing people who can't attend public meetings, can't talk with their elected officials, and don't have the skills to study issues affecting them. Reporters fill those needs. They expose shortcomings, not to make individuals or communities look bad, but because they seek the best for those they represent. Teach them to know the community, its history, its people, its goals. Then work to highlight and help fix whatever is broken, and to celebrate whatever works.

Each level brings challenges for editors. Here are a few with Level 1.

Some editors go ballistic over writers who fall short in writing clean stories.

Don't let those writers set you off. Work with them to identify what they are doing well and where they need to improve. Be specific, realizing that you can't improve everything at one time. Keep training options available including writing exercises, college grammar courses, and teaming them with others who have strengths where they are weak. Maybe you should also check your hiring process. Why are you working with writers who aren't reaching the minimum standards for a story?

Many veteran editors have a list of the common problems in Level 1 reporting.

We asked Jackie Jones about her list. She has been an editor at the *Philadelphia Daily News*, *New York Newsday*, and now at *The Washington Post*. She named three problems of young writers: misspelling, misquoting, and making assertions that aren't supported by facts. She said:

Misspellings usually come from laziness. Reporters often don't use a spell-checker or dictionary because they assume the copy desk will catch errors. If there's time, I'll push a story back and ask the reporter to check it to encourage him to take responsibility for his work.

Misquoting often involves getting some of the words right, but losing the meaning. Ask them about a quote and young reporters will tell you, "That's what they said," but you can tell the quote was taken out of context.

Too often young reporters will assert something happened for reasons that they can't confirm. In the story they'll even accuse someone of fraud or lying without being able to support the charge. Once a reporter wrote about a homeless man who was struck and killed by a bus. She suggested the homeless were more vulnerable to pedestrian accidents although there were no records to support that. Someone in an interview suggested it and she turned it into a fact. I caught it and she changed it. We talked about sources and how to be sure your information is credible.

Level II — The Complete Report

Once writers have mastered the clean report, what's their goal? The next step might be to produce a good read or a well-produced piece. It is concise and well-organized. The goal here is a story that has all the basics of Level I and a professional presentation. The measure of service is that folks understand it and enjoy it.

ROBBER'S EFFORTS STALL

He came armed with a gun and an alien-looking mask shielding his face.

But no disguise or weapon, it seems, could make up for the missing getaway plan of a BurgerWorld robber Tuesday evening.

Police said Jack Cooper, 32, of Clarkville, stepped into the BurgerWorld at First Street and Hunter's Lane about 7:40 p.m. Tuesday. Witnesses said he wore a mask, a blue hooded sweat shirt, and blue jeans.

As store clerks and customers murmured about the man in the strange mask, witnesses said, he bolted to the back of the restaurant and raised a gun.

"He didn't say anything," said Mark Monroe, 18, a store employee.

After getting several bags of money, the man ran out the door with Terry Smith on his trail.

Smith, 23, a salesman at a men's clothing store across the street, had been in the BurgerWorld at the time of the holdup and ran back to his store to call police.

When he saw the robber flee, Smith ran after him for a couple of blocks until police arrived.

Officers caught up to Cooper after he hopped into a Honda he had carjacked from a couple in the Big Store parking lot at Center Mall. The car has a standard transmission, and Cooper couldn't shift gears.

He was charged with armed robbery and carjacking and was held at the county jail Tuesday night.

Checklist for Level II — The Complete Report

All the qualities of Level I and the following:

Organized: The story unfolds in a natural, clear order. Sources appear in ways that don't require repeated identification.

Concise: Each word is needed, each sentence is packed with information.

Enterprising: The story goes beyond a recitation of quotes. The reporting brings in additional information to shed light on positions presented, provide context, and suggest next steps.

Active: Writers know the difference between active and passive, and use the former.

Vigorous: Strong verbs reduce the need for adverbs.

Well-phrased: The writer "turns a phrase" by using alliteration, a pun or a catchy construction. The story offers gold coins such as lively quotes, an anecdote, or interesting facts that encourage readers to stay with the story.

Beware of Level II stories. At 30 seconds or 12 to 20 inches they form the bulk of news reports: the standard story, told the standard way at the standard length. A bored public responds by turning to something else. Look for new ways of storytelling. Use these stories to shatter the notion that good stories must be long. Short writing can and should be excellent writing. Don't skimp on the reporting. Be generous in the reporting but a tightwad in the telling. Know when to settle for a nugget, when to allow longer treatments, and when the story is best told by a graphic, a photo essay, or some other device.

Level III — The Compelling Report

Now we arrive at mastering the craft. This story must be built on earlier layers, but it adds the challenge of moving people to action. Compelling stories grow out of unusual topics or unusual treatment of common topics. They result from depth in reporting, depth that leads to revealing details and interesting anecdotes. The measure of service is the water cooler test. This is the story that people mention around the water cooler or over a meal. They are moved to tell someone about the story. At its highest form, the compelling report moves people to a new understanding or to act on an issue. (See examples below.)

Checklist for Level III — The Compelling Report

Innovative: Writer uncovers a fresh topic or gives an innovative telling to an old story.

Well-paced: Good use of long and short sentences. Emphatic words at the end of sentences. One thought per sentence.

Authoritative: The writer shows the research that allows voice in writing.

Narrative-based: The story has a beginning, middle, and end.

Integrated: The story blends words and visuals, and audio (if the medium allows). The reporter looks for use of photos, graphics or sounds, and works with others to enhance the story.

Structured: The structure, mood, and content agree. Writer thinks through these elements before writing.

Community-minded: The story brings communities into conversation. It helps readers in their role as citizens, helps them better understand themselves and those around them.

Once writers master the basics and advance past complete stories, they're ready to take on techniques of award-winning writing. Novelists and scriptwriters, reporters and copywriters use all kinds of steps to produce lively writing. We'll use some examples of steps that can improve copy for writers at various levels. Writers don't have to do a major project to try some of the techniques. Look for and praise successful uses of techniques in all levels of reports.

<u>Telling Details</u>
ALL SHE HAS, $150,000, IS GOING TO A UNIVERSITY
By Rick Bragg
The New York Times
1996 Pulitzer Prize, Feature Writing
ASNE Award, Non-Deadline Writing

Osceola McCarty spent a lifetime making other people look nice. Day after day for most of her 87 years, she took in bundles of dirty clothes and made them clean and neat for parties she never attended, weddings to which she was never invited, graduations she never saw.

She had quit school in the sixth grade to go to work, never married, never had children and never learned to drive because there was never any place in particular she wanted to go. All she ever had was the work, which she saw as a blessing. Too many other black people in rural Mississippi did not have even that.

She spent almost nothing, living in her old family home, cutting the toes out of shoes if they did not fit right and binding her ragged Bible with Scotch tape to keep Corinthians from falling out. Over the decades, her pay, mostly dollar bills and change, grew to more than $150,000.

"More than I could ever use," Miss McCarty said the other day without a trace of self-pity. So she is giving her money away, to finance scholarships for black students at the University of Southern Mississippi here in her hometown, where tuition is $2,400 a year.

"I wanted to share my wealth with the children," said Miss McCarty, whose only real regret is that she never went back to school. "I never minded work, but I was always so busy, busy. Maybe I can make it so the children don't have to work like I did."

That's the beginning of a story that helped make Miss McCarty a celebrity, and helped Rick Bragg earn major awards. He began with an event that has the strong universal qualities of sacrifice, overcoming odds, and finding meaning in life. The event alone didn't make a great story, though. Many others wrote about Miss McCarty's gift. Bragg told a better story.

Look at his writing. What do we know about Miss McCarty and her gift? More importantly, how do we know these things? Which details allow us to see her, hear her, enter into her mind and her world? Instead of saying "She worked hard all her life," Bragg writes, "Day after day, for most of her 87 years..." Instead of just saying she was very religious and also frugal, he wrote, "She binds her ragged Bible with Scotch tape to keep Corinthians from falling out." That's the difference between showing and telling. How do writers gather telling details? Consider how much of this story required Bragg to visit McCarty's home.

Writers and editors face tough decisions about which details to keep and which to drop. Notice how the details here advance the story. Each tells a fact but also a volume about some aspect of McCarthy's life. Details add color. Specific details allow audiences to draw conclusions. Telling details advance the story. How do you include telling details? Be observant. Visit the person's environment when possible. Look for those things that say something about the person, place, or situation. Get everything in the notes. Then choose the ones that best advance the story.

The Right Moment/The Right Angle

Some call it Conceptual Freshness. It is the ability to see the same thing that everyone else sees, but approach it in a new way. Photojournalists need foresight to predict the revealing image and the patience to wait for the right moment to capture it. So do wordsmiths. KING-TV, Seattle, found a different angle in reporting a dancer's death. During a noon show in a park, one performer stood on a roof producing a haunting sound with a conch shell. Two other performers, suspended by their feet, descended from a roof. Suddenly a supporting rope snapped, and one man fell to his death. The photographer captured the moment when the rope broke, but the story didn't show the man's fatal end. Instead, as the victim fell out of the camera frame, the shot moved to his partner who looked over his shoulder, watching the tragedy.

The anchor's lead-in reported the man's death, but the report told the story in chronological order. A happy lunch-time crowd became shocked witnesses to a death. The sound of the conch shell created a natural, mourning track. Maybe the reporter made the difference. He was an arts reporter. He saw the story differently and told it compellingly.

Others excel in finding the right moment or the right angle. No group is better at finding a fresh approach than National Public Radio. Writers there have engaged listeners with a series of journal entries on being one of Santa's elves in a shopping mall, with images of flood victims, comments on Supreme Court rulings, and e-mail notes from a teenager caught in a war zone. When it seems there's nothing new to be said, NPR finds a way.

Explain the Complex
AMERICA: WHAT WENT WRONG
By Donald L. Barlett and James B. Steele
Philadelphia Inquirer
1991

Worried that you are falling behind, not living as well as you once did? Or expected to?

That you are going to have to work extra hours, or take a second job, just to stay even with your bills?

That the company you have worked for all these years may dump you for a younger person?

Or that the pension you have been promised may not be there when you retire?

Worried, if you are on the bottom rung of the economic ladder, that you will never see a middle-class lifestyle?

Or, if you are a single parent or part of a young working family, that you will never be able to save enough to buy a home?

That you are paying more than your fair share of taxes?

Worried that the people who represent you in Congress are taking care of themselves and their friends at your expense?

You are right. Keep worrying.

For those people in Washington who write the complex tangle of rules by which the economy operates have, over the last 20 years, rigged the game — by design and default — to favor the privileged, the powerful and the influential. At the expense of everyone else.

Seizing on that opportunity, an army of business buccaneers began buying, selling and trading companies the way most Americans buy, sell and trade knickknacks at a yard sale. They borrowed money to destroy, not to build. They constructed financial houses of cards, then vanished before they collapsed.

Caught between the lawmakers in Washington and the dealmakers on Wall Street have been millions of American workers forced to move from jobs that once paid $15 an hour into jobs that now pay $7. If, that is, they aren't already the victims of mass layoffs, production halts, shuttered factories and owners who enrich themselves by doing that damage and then walking away.

As a result, the already rich are richer than ever; there has been an explosion in overnight new rich; life for the working class is deteriorating; and those at the bottom are trapped. For the first time in this century, members of a generation entering adulthood will find it impossible to achieve a better lifestyle than their parents. Most will be unable even to match their parents' middle-class status.

AFFECTED BY WASTE
By Joby Warrick, Pat Stith, and Melanie Sill
The Raleigh News & Observer
1996 Pulitzer Prize, Public Service

Imagine a city as big as New York suddenly grafted onto North Carolina's Coastal Plain. Double it.

114

Now imagine that this city has no sewage treatment plants. All the wastes from 15 million inhabitants are simply flushed into open pits and sprayed onto fields.

Turn those humans into hogs, and you don't have to imagine at all. It's already here.

A vast city of swine has risen practically overnight in the counties east of Interstate 95. It's a megalopolis of 7 million animals that live in metal confinement barns and produce two to four times as much waste, per hog, as the average human.

All that manure — about 9.5 million tons a year — is stored in thousands of earthen pits call lagoons, where it is decomposed and sprayed or spread on crop lands. The lagoon system is the source of most hog farm odor, but industry officials say it's a proven and effective way to keep harmful chemicals and bacteria out of water supplies.

New evidence says otherwise:

The News & Observer has obtained new scientific studies showing that contaminants from hog lagoons are getting into groundwater. One N.C. State University report estimates that as many as half of existing lagoons — perhaps hundreds — are leaking badly enough to contaminate groundwater.

The industry also is running out of places to spread or spray the waste from lagoons. On paper, the state's biggest swine counties already are producing more phosphorous-rich manure than available land can absorb, state Agriculture Department records show.

Scientists are discovering that hog farms emit large amounts of ammonia gas, which returns to earth in rain. The ammonia is believed to be contributing to an explosion of algae growth that's choking many of the state's rivers and estuaries.

The writers in these two stories use some of the best techniques in telling hard stories.

First, they don't ignore the BBIs, boring but important stories. Human interest stories are a natural draw. Stories on babies, deaths, and other losses tug at emotions. Government policies are another matter, and hog manure is about as unappealing a topic as there is. The writers took on the topics, told the stories well, and were rewarded by helping the public understand complex issues. Many of the crucial issues of our time are Boring But Important. Take them on; make them interesting.

Second, they used the known to explain the unknown. One story begins by asking penetrating questions. The other starts by asking readers to ponder that which is conceivable, in order to explain that which is difficult to imagine. Both catch the readers on familiar ground and move them through complex issues.

Third, spread out the numbers. Complex stories often contain a wealth of statistics, numbers that tend to numb readers and viewers. These sections contain a lot of numbers, but they don't hit at one time. That encourages readers to assimilate information and stay with the story.

Know When to Write from the Heart
LOVES WON AND LOST:
FOR BLACK MEN, ONE FROM THE HEART
By Donna Britt
The Washington Post
Valentine's Day Column, 1990

Statistics suggest they are "endangered." Oprah, Geraldo and endless TV specials describe them as "at risk." Movies that deal with them positively portray them as afterthoughts and background music; the rest say they're thieves and abusers, the architects and victims of the drug culture. Their own women, it seems, have turned on them, shouting their failings from the rooftops and the pages of bestsellers.

Even under all that weight, even with so many expectations of awfulness, black men manage to amaze.

I mean, really. Look at Michael Jordan, turning empty air into his personal trampoline. Or Denzel Washington, blending gorgeousness, talent and an almost shimmering sexiness — while retaining his image as a rock-steady family man.

Check out Nelson Mandela, whose amazing grace as he strode into a chaotic future made the outrage of being deprived of 27 vital years seem ennobling.

This is a valentine for black men, from one black woman speaking for a whole lot more. And not just because men of African descent could use a few valentines after so much bad press. It's for their being so good at so many disparate things. For surviving so much. For being bigger and better than the hype could ever suggest.

A SENTIMENTAL JOURNEY TO LA CASA OF CHILDHOOD
By Mirta Ojito
The New York Times
1999 ASNE Award, Covering the World

This is the moment when, in my dreams, I begin to cry. And yet, I'm strangely calm as I go up the stairs to the apartment of my childhood in Santos Suarez, the only place that, after all these years, I still refer to as la casa, home.

I am holding a pen and a reporter's notebook in my hand, and, as I always do when I am working, I count the steps: 20. In my memory, *there were only 16. The staircase seems narrower than I remember, the ceiling lower.*

Perhaps I have grown taller, perhaps my hips have widened with age and pregnancy. I am buying mental time, distracting my mind from what I am certain will be a shock.

After 17 years and 8 months, I have returned to Cuba as a reporter. I am here to cover the visit of Pope John Paul II, not to cry at the sight of a chipped, old tile on the floor.

The last time I went down these steps I was 16 years old and a police car was waiting for me and my family downstairs. They had come to tell us that my uncle, like thousands of other Cuban exiles who had returned to Cuba to claim their relatives, waited at the port of Mariel to take us to Miami in a leased shrimp boat.

It was May 7, 1980, the first days of what became known as the Mariel boat lift, the period from April to September 1980 when more than 125,000 Cubans left the island for the United States.

For Britt, the right time to tell a different story was Valentine's Day. For Ojita, it was a return to Cuba. Both pieces drew huge reader response. We shy away from personal pieces except as columns. Reporters learn early to avoid the word "I" in stories, yet some of the most powerful pieces come from personal expressions. People look for ways to connect with the news. They connect by sharing similar experiences, or just by participating in the human experience. Mirta Ojito said her story drew response in part because everyone relates to the idea of going home. Britt's connected because hers was an unexpected expression of affection. Both offered readers something very different. They moved from the safe detachment of news stories to something up close and human.

Write with Rhythm
AUTISTIC SAVANT
By Bob Brown
20/20

His eyes have seen the world's great cities.
His hands have placed those sights on paper.
If the secret wish of travelers is to have their destinations all to
themselves, in his way he does.
Only God knows what he really sees when he draws or what
breezes blow in the climate of his mind.
Steven Wilcher is autistic.

Reporters don't set out to pen lyrics, but when they get it
right, the writing sings. What gives this excerpt rhythm? Count
the syllables in the segment above. Notice the blend of short passages (7 or 8 syllables) with long passages. Consider the word
choices. Notice the powerful words at the end of phrases.
Sometimes the language flows from us as melodious prose. For
most of us, most of the time it comes after solid reporting, painful
drafting, and tedious editing in which we craft words into music.

Write to the End
Look at the writing from the beginning and end of this next
story.

HIS DREAMS BELONG TO THE NEXT GENERATION
By Diana Griego Erwin
Orange County Register

1990 ASNE Award, Commentary

His brow furrowed and the crow's-feet deepened as he struggled to understand. There was little doubt. He was confused.

The busy information clerk at the Department of Motor Vehicles in Santa Ana didn't notice.

"You need to go over there," she said, pointing across the room to the sea of people waiting. "I already told you."

It was 11 a.m. Her patience was shot for the morning. The man pulled at the waistband of his beige work pants and scratched his sun-aged face. He stared at her, stalling for time as he tried to understand, but afraid to say he didn't.

He left, returned. The next clerk didn't speak Spanish either.

"Why can't they learn English?" she grumbled to me, the next in line.

I asked Luis Manuel Delgado why he waited.

"The lady who speaks Spanish has gone to lunch," he said.

There was no irritation in his voice, no anger at the time wasted. It was simply a fact. I pointed out that the clerks hadn't treated him very nicely. Didn't that anger him? I wondered.

"I should know how to speak English," he said with a quiet simplicity. "This is the United States...."

And in the last section:

"My kids are very good," he said. "They get good marks in school. They speak English. No accent. One wants to be a doctor. When they first came here I told them to study English and learn it well. Don't let them treat you like a donkey like they treat your papa."

I asked him if it didn't hurt, being treated "como un burro," like he *said.*

"No, I am not a donkey and my children know it. They know I do all this for them.

"They are proud of me. Nothing anyone else says or does can make me sad when they have pride in me.

"And they will never be donkeys."

He nodded toward the stressed-out information clerks busily shuffling papers behind the government-issued desk. "And they won't work here," he said. "This is donkey work."

Powerful stories hold audiences to the end. Powerful endings won't come from story leftovers. Writers need to plan, saving something special for the end. They should know the end from the beginning.

Why Some Good Stories Aren't Compelling

Ever had all the pieces of a great story, but the story fell flat? "Disappointing" is not the word. All involved are let down, and many times no one can figure out what went wrong. In many newsrooms no one says anything, as if politely walking around a corpse. Here are common reasons why stories don't make it to their potential.

Missing the Real Meaning

A part of the organization step in the Writing Process is answering the question: What's this story about? That's a focus question. It also has a deeper meaning. Chip Scanlan of The Poynter Institute explains it by quoting an editor whom he faced years ago as a young reporter. Chip had written a story about a blind boy. He had put in a lot of work and felt proud of his story.

He expected compliments from his editor, Joel Rawson, but instead, Rawson got in his face and asked, "What's this story really about?" Rawson was asking, when you get beyond the facts, what's the larger meaning of the story.

Compelling stories have a universal quality. They touch something in the human experience and we respond. Many good stories bring us information, take us to interesting places, show us things we haven't seen before, but they don't move us if they don't touch a universal chord. Some good stories never answer the question: What is this story really about?

Here's how reporter David Von Drehle of *The Washington Post* explained writing a great story by applying this step on deadline at a former president's funeral.

The day of Richard Nixon's funeral was unseasonably cold. The sky was overcast and the air was damp. I don't know why a wet chill goes right to the bone, but it does. Sitting in the press tent, watching the minutes tick away toward deadline, I lost the feeling in my fingers.

But then, deadline always makes me shiver.

My seat was next to the team from The New York Times. Earlier in the day, I watched them arrive with the same sick feeling pitchers experienced watching the '61 Yankees take the field. Maureen Dowd, Johnny Apple, David Margolick — they were so deep in talent they had a Pulitzer Prize winner, William Safire, shagging quotes. So I was cold and I was scared.

At a time like that, you have to fall back on the basics: Sit down and tell a story.

What happened?

What did it look like, sound like, feel like? Who said what? Who did what?

And why does it matter?

What's the point? Why is this story being told? What does it say about life, about the world, about the times we live in?

Newspaper writing, especially on deadline, is so hectic and complicated — the fact gathering, the phrase-finding, the inconvenience, the pressure — that it's easy to forget the basics of storytelling. Namely, what happened, and why does it matter?

I did this story the way I always work on deadline: I wandered and watched and listened and wrote down everything as I waited for the story to emerge. Until I figured out the what and the why, I had no way of knowing what details would prove important.

Then I saw Henry Kissinger, the cerebral Cold Warrior, and Bob Dole, the stoic veteran of World War II, each burst into genuine tears. And I heard Billy Graham speaking of the "democracy of death." It hit me that I was watching one of the oldest and most important stories there is: the leveling effect of death, and the fear, the awe, it inspires. Thomas Gray wrote his famous Elegy in a Country Churchyard on just this theme:

The boast of heraldry, the pomp of power,
And all that beauty, all that wealth e'er gave,
Awaits alike the' inevitable hour,
The paths of glory lead but to the grave.

Once I realized what the story was, I targeted my reporting to find details that would drive it home. The signs of time in the faces of the mourners. The ineffable music floating over the babble. The landscape remade in Nixon's lifetime, by once-powerful, now-forgotten, men and women.

Here's how the story begins:

MEN OF STEEL ARE MELTING WITH AGE
By David Von Drehle
The Washington Post
1994 ASNE Finalist, Deadline Reporting

YORBA LINDA, Calif. — When last the nation saw them all together, they were men of steel and bristling crew cuts, titans of their time—which was a time of pragmatism and ice water in the veins.

How boldly they talked. How fearless they seemed. They spoke of fixing their enemies, of running over their own grandmothers if it would give them an edge. Their goals were the goals of giants: Control of a nation, victory in the nuclear age, strategic domination of the globe.

The titans of Nixon's age gathered again today, on an unseasonably cold and gray afternoon, and now they were white-haired or balding, their steel was rusting, their skin had begun to sag, their eyesight was failing. They were invited to contemplate where power leads.

Overwriting

Picture the speaker who rises to address a large, diverse, uninterested group. From his first words he captures the audience. His fiery speech engrosses them. His command of the subject impresses them. His dramatic flair engages them. They follow his every word.

But by the second hour, they've worn out. The speaker is just as fiery, with just as much command of subject and he still has a dramatic flair, but he has simply outlasted his audience.

Thus is the fate of many stories. They're wonderful; they just go on too long. Granted, the public has only so much time to attend to the news, but we're not talking about an issue of available time. Great reports will cause people to find the time. The problem of overwriting is not that people didn't have the time; they just have had more than they could take of a good thing. The solution: use the cream from the top. Save the rest for a later book or documentary.

Overwriting also refers to inflated language. It is the tearjerker built around evocative language rather than facts. It is the sentence readers know is unrue, the overstatement that passes by the editor. Consider the story of a traffic accident one rainy night. Traffic is backed up in long columns of frustrated headlights. A cluster of emergency vehicles assembles, red, ellow, blue and white lights flashing. It is quite a sight, and it impresses the reporter. The next morning readers are served the following: "You might have thought a spaceship had landed on West Boulevard last night." No, you wouldn't. Strunk and White call it the use of "ornate prose" that ought to be avoided. Overwriting is also the forced metaphor, simile, or other analogy that occurs when the writer is straining for cleverness.

The answer to overwriting is simple: just make the point and end the story. Better to underwrite by a bit than overwrite.

Failure to Deliver

This is the opposite of telling too much. The story doesn't live up to its billing because the reporting doesn't support the case. Perhaps the reporter has a wealth of interesting threads but can't tie them together. That leaves interesting stuff, not a great story. Most editors learn to face the pressure from short-circuiting a project. They reward the writer for good work done and tell the higher ups the story didn't work out, rather than burdening the public with an unconvincing story. Don't publish your mistakes.

Editors sometimes wonder whether they should seek to make every story compelling. Probably not. Some stories merit only a few simple paragraphs, but those graphs should be clear and complete. For example, meteorologists predict another day of clear skies and high temperatures. How high? Road construction will slow traffic on the interstate. Where's the detour? Good writers search for the lever that lifts every story above the ordinary, but every story doesn't have to be, can't be, exceptional.

Some wonder whether compelling stories require a lot of time. They don't have to be time-consuming. Many award-winning daily stories confirm the notion that writers can produce good stories on deadline. In fact, journalists face a special challenge today in producing compelling stories quickly. The Internet demands it. Audiences for big breaking news stories require it. Society needs to understand complex, breaking stories. That calls for journalists who can tell compelling stories on deadline. Speed is important, but that's only one side of the story. The other side is that some stories take time and space. You, as editor, have to find time for writers to work on compelling stories. If you say you want excellence, you'll have to find ways to give writers the time needed.

Many newsroom leaders act as though one or two select reporters are the only ones who can produce compelling stories. Everyone should be expected to rise to that level and everyone deserves a chance. The most talented writers will respond regularly, but encourage others, too.

Editors wrestle with the challenge of working with the reporter who has done everything. We suggest that you find new challenges. Mix long, meaty stories, with daily pieces. Vary the topics. Try different beats. Reward good work by allowing experiments, but then regularly return to some work in general reporting. Call on the great writers to be teachers, mentors, and editors. Just don't ignore them. One of editing's worst sins is to have a newsroom where reporters get good enough to be ignored.

One study of journalists over 40 says they continue to yearn for great stories, and they want a sense of progression in their work.[11] Most said they have good relations with their editors, but they are frustrated because those editors are often too green or too busy to help them. If you're editing writers whose craft skills exceed yours, find an avenue that allows them to grow. Find another guide or special training so they can continue to learn. And catch up.

Teaching Through Levels

Story levels offer several devices to help you as a teacher. They allow you and the staff to define expectations for stories, and they provide a shorthand. That helps in evaluating stories. Story levels also help in performance reviews and in charting career paths. A writer might ask to do more big stories. You as editor can explain that the person needs to show a greater mastery of Level I skills. The two of you can go over stories and look at strengths and weaknesses.

You might decide on a different terminology for story types, or you might prefer a different approach, but do something that allows you to talk about story quality. Several editors have chosen the terminology, "It stinks." Somehow that's not as helpful in

---

[11] "In Their Prime: Motivating Senior Reporters," by Sharon L. Peters, NMC Executive Education Research and Partnership, Northwestern University, 1997.

guiding writers to the next step. As you choose the language, you can improve the conversation in the newsroom, and improve the quality of work.

Editors Keep Growing

To be an effective teacher you must continue to learn. Here are a few suggestions.

Read widely: Forget the book of the month. That's great if you have the time, but most likely you don't. How about a book each quarter? Set a reading goal of at least 15 minutes each day. A book will take awhile at that rate, but you will have read at least four books each year. Vary your reading. Read one book on writing, followed by something that's not about craft. Try a classic or a best-selling novel, a sci-fi or romance paperback, then something meaningful like history, philosophy, or sociology to make up for the paperback. Review the book list in Chapter 3. Read The Elements of Style once a year. It has fewer than 100 pages. Some books offer specific tips for storytelling; others will fuel your creativity, expand your knowledge, and relax you after a long day.

Look for Writing Ideas in the Arts: Various forms offer lessons for your job. Consider concise writing in poetry, rhythm in writing from music, presenting characters in theater, structure in a movie, detail in sculpture, the senses in paintings, and others.

Get Training: Attend at least one major training session each year. Consider writing/editing workshops, seminars, and college courses. Press clubs, media institutes, foundations, and universities offer programs that will refresh you. Your example will do more than anything you say to encourage a learning newsroom.

Teach a Formal Session: Your job calls on you to teach individuals every day, but plan some occasions when you teach a group.

Do it in your newsroom, maybe as a brown bag lunch. Accept an invitation to teach a session in a college course, at a high school or even an elementary school. You'll be surprised how much you learn. Teaching forces you to organize and articulate your thoughts.

Chart a Course of Study and Follow It: Set some learning goals. Do you understand each point of the checklists in this chapter? Can you give a good 2-minute lesson on active and passive verbs? Do you understand voice in writing? What are your hidden knowledge gaps? Do something about them.

Write Regularly: Remind yourself of the painful sweetness of composition. Periodically report and write something. Let others see your writing, and get their advice. Try new approaches and ask someone to edit your work.

Write for Yourself: Consider a journal or another form of private writing to keep your senses sharp.

We'll end with words from an outstanding writing teacher. Roy Peter Clark, senior scholar at the Poynter Institute, says writers learn in four ways:

By writing;
By reading about writing;
By reading writers;
By talking about reading and writing.

Those are the direct ways. The indirect ways are by going to the movies, studying photography, visiting a museum, listening to music, taking music lessons, or taking a cooking class.

He also offers this list of ways of reading copy for writers and editors:

Reading for voice;
Reading for voices;
Reading for accuracy;
Reading for holes;
Reading for clutter;
Reading for language;
Reading for information;
Reading for experience;
Reading for altitude;
Reading for structure;
Reading for clarity;
Reading for comprehensibility;
Reading for coherence;
Reading for cohesion;
Reading for audience;
Reading for inclusion;
Reading for purpose;
Reading for consequences;
Reading for mobility;
Reading for detail;
Reading for pace;
Reading for emphasis;
Reading for conversation;
Reading for numbers;
Reading for impact;
Reading for color;
Reading for flow.

When you can explain and have your newsroom practicing each of these, you may grade yourself a master teacher.

THE JOY OF A CRAFT THAT CAN NEVER BE LEARNED

By Donald M. Murray, from his book Write to Learn: Fourth Edition

You have explored a craft that can never be learned. Be grateful — writing will bring you a lifetime of discovery and surprise. I have been writing for the 50 years since I was 17, but each morning at my writing desk I am again 17. I face the page with just enough fear to make it exciting and little enough expectation to allow me to write what I do not expect.

Writing has allowed my voice to be heard. I have been able to participate in our society, arguing for new ways to teach writing, arguing against old ways of resolving differences and against war, speaking out on the satisfactions and concerns of my generation. At my writing desk, I have been able to discover and explore the mysteries of life and survive the tragedies that enter each life — hurt and loss, sickness and death. I have been able to complain and to celebrate, mourn and laugh, imagine and learn.

Writing has also brought me the gift of concentration as I become lost in my craft, searching for the right word, creating the phrase that gives off sparks of meaning, constructing sentences that flow and paragraphs that satisfy, tuning the music of my voice to my evolving meaning.

Readers have told me that I have articulated their feelings and their thoughts and in that way have made me a voting member of the human community.

Writing began as play and it has remained play. I hope you will be as fortunate and find a lifetime of play in fooling around with language and finding yourself surprised by unintended meaning.

CHAPTER SEVEN
Coaching Writers

Deadline nears. The copy comes in and it's a mess. The clock ticks. You do the only thing you can: fix the story. Quietly you're proud that your reporting and editing skills allow you to save the story. You're also pleased with the story the public will see. You've done the right thing. You plan to have a talk with the reporter about the changes tomorrow.

Now it is tomorrow. Deadline nears. The copy comes in and it's a mess. The clock ticks....

What's an overworked editor to do?

You coach. It is the best way we know for you not merely to survive but thrive.

Coaching is a style of newsroom leadership that says focusing on people brings a greater return than focusing on what they produce, although obviously the two cannot be separated. If you help the people, they will improve the work. In the news business that means you improve the journalism by improving the writers.

Along the way, you also improve the newsroom atmosphere. That might extend the news careers of staff who get tired of the tension and lack of growth.

In the book, *Coaching Writers*, Roy Peter Clark and Don Fry[12] explain that coaching goes against traditional newsroom conduct. Usually editors fix copy because that's quick and efficient. Unfortunately, you must do it day after day after day. Coaching works because if you invest some time with the writer early, you'll save time in the long run. That's consulting with the writer early in the story process, and early in your writing/editing relationship. Good use of front-end work saves trouble later. It doesn't always work, but it does usually work, with persistence.

A second difference is in communications. Newsrooms typically communicate poorly. A common cry of reporters is, "I never hear anything from my editor." Many are so turned off by arbitrary changes that they shrink from the editor's comments. Many editors, tired of quarrelsome reporters, fix the story and skip the comments. Coaching is built on talking to each other about stories. It means writers and editors discussing what works in a story and what needs work. Coaching brings writers and editors together working toward the same goal.

Getting Started

Maybe your newsroom has a healthy learning environment. Count yourself lucky. Most don't. If yours doesn't, why don't you start coaching? Nothing's stopping you. To be a newsroom coach, focus on four steps:

Let the writer maintain ownership of the story;

---

[12] *Coaching Writers*, St. Martin's Press, New York NY, 1992.

Ask useful questions;

Listen;

Look for areas to praise as well as areas of concern.

It helps you if writers feel ownership of their stories. Reporters know how it feels to craft a story, take it to the editor, and watch the editor just take it over. The editor dives in, editing out words and phrases, asking questions that are answered in the paragraphs she has not yet read. The writer stands by, seething.

Coaching would have the editor read the whole piece first, keep her fingers off the keys, and edit more by talking than typing. That way the writer retains some control. The editor guides, the writer responds. Together they improve the story.

The conversation at the computer is not about what the editor thinks should be done. The editor is not pointing out line by line changes that she could have more quickly made herself. Instead the conversation is based on useful questions to advance the story. Here are some:

How's it going? (Over time, writers learn you are there to help with specifics, not to get a general progress report.)

What's next?

What's your focus?

How will you end the piece?

What's the top of the story?

What works?

What needs work?

What worries you here?

What do you like best?

COACHING WRITERS

Adapted from Coaching Writers *by Roy Peter Clark and Don Fry*

WHAT IS COACHING?

A way to improve newswriting by helping journalists do their best work. It focuses on improving the writers instead of improving the copy.

HOW DOES COACHING DIFFER FROM FIXING?

Fixing	Coaching
a) focuses on the editor's control	a) focuses on the writer's growth
b) leads to dependence and frustration	b) builds the writer's confidence
c) solves immediate problems, but must be repeated again and again	c) takes longer initially, but frees editor and writer over time
d) sets individual against individual	d) encourages teamwork

WHAT MUST THE EDITOR/COACH DO?

- Listen intently
- Encourage the writer by looking for areas to praise
- Ask useful questions
- Help the writer develop the piece while leaving ownership with the writer

PERSONAL GOALS

Improve the communications to improve the journalism

Take responsibility for your growth

Look for newsroom heroes/heroines and learn from them

AN INVENTORY

- How does an editor or writer help you do your best work?
- How does that person hinder your best efforts?
- How do you help that person?
- What would that person like you to change about the way you work

The questions reinforce important elements of writing. They should help the writer think more clearly about the story. As you coach, you will learn which questions are most helpful to which writers. Your goal is to ask questions that encourage the writer to think aloud about strengths and weaknesses, as well as to give you a sense of how the story is going. Good questions propel a writer to the finish. Ask questions that assist.

Learn to listen to the writer. This is a rare skill, and editors who think they are doing it often are not. Ask some editors whether they have a coaching newsroom, and they say, "Oh, yeah." Ask the writers in the same newsroom, and they say, "Nope." The newsroom has the form but not the substance of coaching. Editors ask questions, but the questions contain the answers: "Don't you think this paragraph should be the lead?" The editing objective is really to manipulate the writer to where the editor wants him to go. Writers see this instantly, of course, and resent it.

The pay-off for good questions and careful listening is that the writer — most writers — will actually talk to you about the story's problems, once they have decided that this isn't just some new management toy. So you have to learn how to listen.

For most of us, listening is an acquired skill. It takes discipline to listen with an open mind rather than occupying the time marshaling arguments against whatever point is being made. It takes discipline to listen to the reporter talk about the story, when you are already late with your contributions to the weekend story budget.

Do you really listen? Are you focused on the writer or are you editing other stories, shouting across the newsroom, and answering the phone? You can coach a story in about two minutes, but you have to spend those two minutes with the writer.

Where do you coach? At your desk? At writers' desks? Can others hear you? Sometimes you want them to. When staffers eavesdrop, you are teaching them, too. Use your judgment; some of these conversations should be private. Where are you, physically, in relation to the writer? Side-by-side coaching reinforces the notion of a team.

What do you praise and what do you express concern about? There's something good in every story. Spot it, but beware of the automatic "but," as in, "I liked your lead, but..." Reporters will wince at that one, which has all the sincerity of you telling a bill collector it's good to see him.

How do you raise problems in coaching? Directly and constructively.

For example:

You've got quite a few spelling errors in this story. How do you think that happened?

The facts are here, but I'm not sure of the focus. What is it? How can you make it clearer?

This story has wonderful elements, but it doesn't move me. Any ideas on how you can increase the impact?

You might also wonder whether coaching deprives you of teaching on deadline. If you have raised elements of good writing in advance, deadline coaching is a good time to explore concepts in your staff's stories.

You might ask:

Remember how we talked about your use of pacing? How could you improve the pace of this piece?

The question leaves the writer to think of a different approach. And the writer might reject your comments. If there's a good reason, fine. If the writer is being obstinate (and a few will be), you can always pull rank. There's an old newsroom saying to the effect that 20 minutes before deadline the newsroom becomes an absolute monarchy.

Next Steps in Coaching

For best effect, coaching occurs at three stages of the Writing Process: at the idea stage, at the end of reporting, and finally at the editing stage. The goal is to avoid late surprises. At the idea stage the writer and editor come together on the preliminary focus. Your questions might be:

What do you hope for?

What's new in the situation?

Your writer returns from an assignment. "What's it looking like?" you ask. Good questions train writers to figure out early what they've got. A reporter who knows she will be expected to spit out a pithy summary to a busy editor learns to focus. This is when you learn whether you are going to get what you thought you were going to get. Often, you're not. Reality close to deadline rarely matches the airy expectations you had that morning. Find out now what's real.

Coaching at the editing stage should be polishing. Period.

"What about time?" you ask. "I hardly have time to read a story through once. How could I coach each story three times?" Well, what happens is that the more you coach, the more writers start coaching themselves, and each other.

Your 10-12 familiar questions start to lodge in people's heads, and they get asked even when you are not there. As people get more understanding of the requirements of each step of the writing process, they gain more control of their work. The quality goes up. Give yourself some time to practice the process, then see how much more efficient you become.

The next matter is coaching the big picture. The process doesn't stop when the story is finished. Use the process to understand your staff's strengths and weaknesses. Track the work of individual reporters. Where are they improving? Which problems seem to trip them repeatedly? Tell them your thoughts. This shouldn't come across as a report card; it should be a way the two of you work on improving.

Remember the coaching process can also be used in performance reviews. This is long coaching. At some point, the two of you take the time to talk through a person's work for the year or some other period of time. The same type of questions help the writer think through his performance and allow you a chance to agree, disagree, and bring in new information.

Ultimately the affect of coaching in a newsroom should move beyond editors and designated coaches. Your goal is a newsroom in which writers and editors collaborate. They share ideas and coach each other: writers to writers, including editors in the role of writers. They've learned how to respond in ways that help the writer. And writers always need help.

Here's how one young reporter learned about collaboration:

DEATH OF A DEMIGOD
By Jim Naughton,
Poynter President

He was the most gifted professional I knew. A consummate reporter. A nurturing boss. A complete bureaucrat. A caring colleague. It was easy to be in awe of him, and I was. Now it was going to become difficult to live with.

The editor was about to join me, for several days, in coverage of the political campaign I was following. He would be sitting next to me on the press plane, eating the same sterile airline food, reading the same handouts—and watching me write. Oh, God. How could I possibly get through the week?

As luck would have it—and if nothing else, I have been greatly fortunate—it was he who had to write first. He joined the campaign with a notebook full of some Washington development or other and had to write about it, typewriter perched on his knees, before we hit the next campaign stop aboard the plane.

So he rolled the paper into the typewriter, just as I would. He sat motionless for several minutes, just as I would. He typed a bit and rolled the platen up and mulled, just as I would. He xxxxed and mmmmed with ferocity, just as I would. He anguished, just as I would.

And then he did an astonishing thing. He asked me to read, over his shoulder, his raw copy.

Dumbly, I read. He had a word in the second graf that was not quite correct. I meekly suggested a replacement. His eyes lit up, and he rolled the copy back down to that spot and inserted my word. My word!

The experience recurred several times before he was finished. And when he had completed the story, he sighed. I looked at him—quizzically, I'm sure. And he said something that, in my naiveté, I thought he had coined at that very moment and realized only years later had been a citation of Dorothy Parker:

"I hate to write, but I love having written."

It summed up my whole existence. And I loved Max Frankel for having let me see, for the first time in my life, that I was not uniquely insecure as a writer.

The demigod was merely human. Thank God.

We end this section with a few notes to remind you of your roles as writer, editor, teacher and coach.

Informal Editing Techniques to Help You Teach, Every Day

First Principles

You are trying to work yourself out of a job. That means you must be thinking constantly of showing people how to do something, rather than doing it yourself. Your primary job is to help other people to succeed.

You are a leader and a manager. Leaders set direction and inspire and motivate. Managers ensure that processes do happen.

What to Bring to the Newsroom Floor

Stand for something. It might be urgency. It might be first-class writing. In a newsroom with a rough history, it might be humane treatment of people. Decide what you stand for and find the language and behavior to express it.

Master the language of stories and news. The Elements of Style can be helpful for this, along with *Coaching Writers.* If you talk with exactness about our work, your reporters will eventually follow suit. Don't say, "it doesn't grab me." Do say, "Notice that verb, and the long dependent clause? What can we do to stiffen that sentence?"

Core Practices

ALWAYS read any story, all the way. Before you talk about

changes, read the whole story. Sounds obvious, but many editors plunge in.

The writer wins the close calls. If you habitually microedit, your writers will dread dealing with you. It's not your story.

Repeat yourself. Be patient with repetition of the essential principles of good reporting and good writing. Most problems with most stories are basic.

Never send a reporter away empty-handed. If asked, "Got a minute?" have one. You can get a lot done in 120 seconds. Many editors make themselves unapproachable, by exuding stress and busyness. You can't teach if people can't get near you.

Bruise hard, heal easy. If your feelings are easily hurt, they will be.

Emphasize the writer. Your job is to help the writer; it is not to take over the story. Good editors help writers. That does not mean you wave garbage through; it means you work with the writer.

Keep it funny. Remember your sense of humor. Writing is a wacky business.

Floor Techniques

Demonstration edit. Edit one paragraph, explaining your actions as you go. Then ask the reporter to give all the paragraphs similar treatment.

Endless repetition. Become known for a handful of things you say, a lot.

Keep the monkey off your back. Pick others' brains. When someone asks you what to do, ask, "What do you recommend?" Not always, but get everybody in the solutions business.

Act confident, even when you are not. This includes having the confidence to say you don't yet know what you think.

"What went right" debrief. Make the reporter the hero, and you'll get more information about what went wrong. Useful question: What would you do differently?

Deciding whether to do a story. What is the least we'll get? The most?

Get people to outline. Call them guides, not outlines. For the reporter who resists even that: "Show me your key points."

When you read copy: Look for "there are," "of the," and "by" as signs of wordy sentences. Teach reporters to look for those phrases, and you start teaching a reporter how to self-edit.

Watch your mouth. Don't blurt, because you'll waste too much time cleaning up after yourself. Rewire yourself so that potential blurts go from impulse to your head and only then to your mouth.

Big ears. Do your editing and talking about stories on the floor, as much as you can, so that people can overhear you. Journalists who don't seem to be listening are. Use judgment here; some conversations need to be private.

Abstract a story. Formally, with a printout and notations in the margin, or informally, just skimming on the tube, talking about what you are getting from what you are reading, as the reporter listens. "What I get from this is..." "No, that's not what I meant at all." Or, "That's it exactly!"

Start nice. The first thing you say after you've read the story shouldn't be critical. It doesn't have to be a lie either. Even on a messy story, you could say: "This was a tough one to write." Or, "Here's what I got from the story. You tell me if that's what you meant." Or, "This guy gave you a great quote." Or, "Looks like you made a lot of calls on this one."

Finger-pointing. Put your finger on the tube and point to a sentence: "This one makes me uneasy," for a sentence you don't understand.

Avoid the invidious comparison. "So-and-so is the best reporter I've ever seen...." You just trashed every other reporter.

Paper the room. Have a book, a chapter, a photocopied page ready, always. Pass this stuff out freely, but not en masse. That is, use a rifle, not a shotgun. Better to have people asking for copies, sounding slightly aggrieved, than to flood the place with paper that is ignored.

THE WRITING COACH IN THE BROADCAST NEWSROOM
By Jill Geisler
The Poynter Institute
Former news director, WITI, Milwaukee

Good newsrooms treasure good writing. Every employee in the shop understands the importance of the written word. Managers develop systems to grow good writers. Scripts are faithfully checked before broadcast. But who is checking the scripts? How are they doing it? Are they fixing copy, or are they doing something much more valuable: Are they coaching writers?

Let's take a common newsroom situation. A reporter has finished writing a package and is ready for a script-check. You are the coach. Here's what you need to do:

• Sit on your hands.

Writers need to know you respect their ownership of a story. Resist the temptation to start writing an improved version. That's fixing — not coaching. (The only exception to this is a critical deadline situation. Even then, ask the writer for permission to lay your hands on the copy.)

• Ask the reporter to tell you about the story.

This is the "content conversation." Listen to how the reporter relates the information. What was the first thing said? What tense was used? In what order were the facts laid out? When was a surprise revealed? What emotion was expressed and when? How did the story end?

• Read the story with a dual personality.

Read the story as a person who knows all the facts (since you just heard them) and as a person who knows nothing more than what the text states.

• Ask the writer — and yourself — questions.

Keep in mind that the writer may be feeling very nervous at this moment. Do your best to be positive as you ask about story elements that are missing, conflicting, confusing, or superfluous. Remember to respect the writer's effort. But often a story that sounded good in the content conversation gets lost in the writing. What changed? Does the text you've read appear to be as strong as the story you've heard?

• Beware of "projected content."

Often writers know the facts of a story so well they presume those facts are in the copy when they aren't. This is when the coach's constructive questions (and mastery of dual-personality copy review) can help the writer see and correct gaps in a story.

• Apply ethical decision-making skills.

Coaching conversations provide excellent opportunities to reinforce journalistic values. Talk about fairness, perspective, diversity, and balance. Again, think in terms of questions: Are there other people we should hear from? Are we telling the story in context?

• Remember the value of legitimate praise.

We all thrive on positive reinforcement. Coaches identify successes and point them out. Even when a story is in great need of repair, its writer may have done a good job of fact-gathering. Acknowledge that. Be specific and genuine when you praise.

• Recognize the difference between "rescue" and "redecoration."

"Rescues" are emergency measures, usually performed to correct factual errors. "Redecoration" is the art of making copy more attractive. It is the majority of what writing coaches do. "Redecorating" is best done when there is plenty of time for consultation and conversation. Don't "redecorate" on deadline.

• Check your ego.

When you "fix" stories by doing instant re-writes, there may be a thrill in showing off your skill. By coaching writers you discover better ways to craft copy. People compliment the writer on a good story, rarely the coach. Your satisfaction comes from knowing the valuable role you play in the professional development of your colleagues and your newsroom.

Good newsrooms treasure good writing. Good writers treasure good coaches.

Section IV
Leadership Skills for Today and Tomorrow

CHAPTER EIGHT
The Candid Editor: Straight Talk

You won't learn how to be candid overnight, and nor should you try. But you should learn it. A reasonable goal is to learn to be candid within two years of becoming an editor. If that sounds easy, it is not, at least for most people.

Set this important goal: I will develop the habit of candor, seasoned with judgment. I will become an editor people count on for honesty, delivered with tact.

You probably know editors who have never learned this. The discomfort of plain talk to another person is just too difficult for them. Plain talk is difficult, but it becomes easier with practice.

This chapter is about talking straight with people, in small ways and large. People fear straight talk, yet they crave it, too. But if the candor does not come from someone who cares for the person on the receiving end, the chances are small that it will be received well.

Think of yourself. There almost certainly have been times when someone has talked with you bluntly, to your own ultimate benefit. It was not an encounter you enjoyed, strictly speaking, yet you are glad it happened, because it did you good.

Keep those talks in mind, for they can be powerful models for you as you struggle to be usefully direct.

Assuming you have a reasonably healthy psyche, you get more

pleasure from being praised than reproved. You also get more pleasure from giving praise than reproof. But you are an editor, and occasional reproofs go with your job. So do those occasions when you tell your boss something she is not, strictly speaking, dying to hear.

You need to learn to level with people, without leveling them. You need to be direct, while conveying the sense of an arm around the shoulder of the person you are talking with. This goes for peers and bosses, too.

Without question, tactless candor can rattle people and damage their confidence. Editors are in the confidence business, and they must be conservators of the sense of common purpose that is the life force of any good organization. But candor need not be a blunt instrument.

To deal with people straightforwardly is a skill. You weren't born with it, and the chances are reasonable that when you became an editor you still had things to learn.

So do many editors, including people who have been on the job for longer than you have. Think of the kind of talk that goes on in your organization.

Typically, two kinds of supervisory conversations prevail: What editors say to staff members and what they say about them.

When editors talk in private about people they supervise, the going is easy. They can blow off a little steam and vent their frustrations. After all, the person they are being so blunt about isn't in the room.

Those same editors, talking to the person in question, often find it extraordinarily difficult to achieve simple, helpful candor. They beat about the bush, utter some vague words, and often leave the recipient baffled, and angry.

An editor needs to prepare for a candid conversation just as a reporter needs to plan a story or a photographer needs to compose a picture. If you begin with careful preparation for the conversations that scare you, the habit of forethought will gradually make you a more thoughtful supervisor.

If you want the respect of the people who work for you, they must know you will level with them, including when it is uncomfortable for you both. You need respect more than you need affection, although it's better to have both.

If you know how to prepare for a big conversation, then you know how to prepare for a little one. And little conversations held early often eliminate the need for bigger ones later. Preparation, too, will help your confidence. If you are confident, you are less likely to convey an air of things being worse than they really are.

Learn how to have the big direct conversation. Then take those skills of preparation and sensitivity and apply them to smaller venues.

Once you do this a half-dozen times, you are on your way to forthrightness.

So think of such conversations in three ways: What you do beforehand, what you do during the conversation and what you do once it is over.

Before

Begin with some reflection.

You know that no editor succeeds while her staff fails. You want your people to succeed, and you know they can. That must be one of your articles of faith. You must convey that confidence, even in a tough conversation. So think about your tone, your expression.

Think about your history, about those times when someone talked some tough sense to you, yet left you feeling hopeful. How did she do it?

Think about your own state of mind. You have hopes and fears, and they play endlessly in your mind. Keep your hopes for your people at center stage, not your fears.

Ask yourself what you are trying to accomplish. What would success in this conversation look like?

Question your assumptions. Are you being fair? What do you know about this person? If there is a file, study it. Is this a cocky 25-year-old with talent and carelessness? A veteran bruised by the years? Who is this person, and how can you reach him?

Focus on the behavior, not the person. This is crucial. You do not want the message to be, "You are a bad person." You want the message to be, "You can do better."

Do your homework. Use facts and specific examples of the behavior that concerns you. Make your case, and then make his case. That is, understand as well as you can how it may look to him. Keep things in proportion. Don't, for example, cite a long litany of transgressions just to prove you know what you're talking about. Don't use a sledgehammer in the name of thoroughness. Beware the sweeping statement.

Candid conversations often go on the rocks because you give voice to suspicions, not observations. Don't go farther than is fair. Remember how it would feel to you to be on the receiving end.

Think of a few key words to make sure you make the points you think are important. Rehearse, alone or with a fellow editor. Strive for balance. Do not psychoanalyze, and do not be a parent. You are a professional talking with a fellow professional.

Have some solutions in mind to offer, if in the course of the talk that seems appropriate. Is it a deadline problem? Have some solutions that other people have found useful. Have a photocopy of some other writer's account of learning to work faster. Always bring something helpful to a tough conversation.

A word about timing. Have these kind of conversations early in the work week. That way, you can check back to head off mis-understandings. If you give someone a tough time on the last day of the week, they have the weekend to brood, without access to you. Have these conversations by Wednesday.

During

Be cordial, but get to the point. Open with a question, if you like: How do you think things are going? Or, something like, "Fred, what happened with that story the other night?" Chances are good that Fred knows exactly which story you mean, which is an implicit acknowledgment of a problem. Chances are also pretty good that if you don't think things are going well, Fred knows that and may acknowledge it in his reply.

Ask questions. Get information. Learn how it looks from Fred's point of view, even if you are cast-iron certain you know all there is to know.

Commiserate where that seems appropriate, but remember why you are in the room. Say what you need to say and say it clearly. Understand that no matter how clearly you say it, the chances are quite good that the message will be only half-heard. You might ask Fred to tell you, in his own words, what he has heard you say.

Do not be surprised if his version bears only a casual relation-ship to what you believe you just said. This means you have the opportunity and obligation to restate your concern. Again, ask

Fred to tell you what he has heard you say.

If things are getting tense, you can say something like, "Fred, I'm not insisting that you agree with me. I just want to be certain I am being clear." Do ask, "What do you think about what you've heard me say?" People are rarely convinced against their will. If you are far apart, you may need to limit your goal to saying what you intend to say clearly and verifying that Fred has heard it and is thinking. If you don't back someone into a corner, it is amazing how much thinking goes on long after the talk that triggered it is over.

That is not the best objective. What you really want is agreement and a plan to fix the problem, but you may need to settle for something less than that.

Finally, do ask, "How can I help?" Say, "I'm your editor. What do you need from me?"

After

You may find that things are a little strained with the person you talked with. You are the senior partner in this relationship, so it's your responsibility to take the initiative to make things right.

Approach the person. Ask how things are going. Check to see if there are any questions, and answer them. Convey a sense of good will.

Do not be surprised if Fred needs reassurance. You may think the conversation was just a mild reproof for some sloppy reporting. Fred, however, may have heard, "Go away! We hate you!"

That is why it is important to have these talks midweek, when people have access to you. If the conversation takes place on a Friday, your staffer has all weekend to imagine the worst.

If you've negotiated a plan for improvement, follow up. If

there's improvement, praise it. If there's not, find out why, and keep the subject on the table.

Keep your promises. If you said you would do something with or for this person, do it. Nail your commitment into your calendar, and deliver.

Most people want to do well. For them to understand what that means, you and other editors must be tireless in articulating and exemplifying your organization's values. The better that people understand those values, the less time you need spend having difficult conversations.

You are an editor, so you have a good pulpit for talking about values, and good work, and high standards. Every meeting is a chance to reinforce. So is every encounter on the floor, every story conference.

Use those occasions, and talk about your newsroom's standards. "Here's a fine piece of work because..." "This is a good story because..." Talk about what you expect.

The last thing you want is for someone to do substandard work because she thinks the standards are lower than they actually are.

You owe people candor. Providing is not easy, nor is it impossible. When you level with someone, you have the satisfaction of knowing that you have done your best to be honest, for the benefit of your organization and the person with whom you are talking.

CHAPTER NINE
Going the distance

You will learn, within a year or two of becoming an editor, whether your heart is in it. There may be a moment that tells you, but more likely there will be a gradual growing into the role, so that your judgments and actions lose some of their early tentativeness, and you begin to enjoy the sense of being responsible for something beyond yourself.

You may begin thinking of those you supervise as "my people." Be careful with such language, even if the phrase springs into mind. You will relish the signs that you have begun to learn your new craft. You'll notice fewer glances of silent exasperation, you won't be in such a hurry to make a decision, you'll begin to acquire habits of seeking advice and following a reasonable due process with those you supervise.

You'll learn that what you and your staff decide to do has lots of impact on people elsewhere in your organization, and you'll learn the things to consult about beforehand and the things simply to inform others about. You'll feel less frustration with the complexities of operating in concert with others, more satisfaction. On good days things will feel as they ought, like life on a team.

People will begin to accept your direction, and it feels not like something you deserve but like a blessing. "Good gosh, they're following me!" Shocking, isn't it? It feels good, too.

You'll spend less time fretting about the way people ought to be, and be more inclined to deal with people as they are. You won't marvel so much at the disheveled condition of much of the copy that arrives on your desk. Instead, you'll be thinking of the process that produced it, and thinking of ways to intervene, for the long run.

You'll get more or less abreast of the paperwork and the cyberwork and the face-to-face work, marveling that it can take so much time and energy to get so little done. If only it weren't for all those other people....

But you'll accept that as a fact of organizational life. You'll begin to see that the point of a workplace is the belief that people will get more done working together than working alone. In that sense, your work life is a nonstop meeting, and on a good day it is a good meeting.

Where do you go from here?

You keep learning. This takes three main forms, and it starts with people:

You continually improve your understanding of human beings, including yourself;

You broaden and deepen your view of the organization and its community;

You strengthen the craft skills that probably were the first things that recommended you for the editing position.

Studying People

Their study is your first priority, ahead even of your need to become an ever more deft story editor. You are primarily in the business of editing people, not just prose. If you relish the nonstop contact this implies, and continue to work to understand your fellows, you will succeed, in the long run. The editor who is a keen student of human behavior is likely to be more effective with people than the editor who overlooks the individuals who actually do the work.

When supervising editors fail, it is usually because of clumsiness with, or indifference to, the people around them. Think of your complaints about your supervisors, past and present. Set aside questions about objectives, such as profit margins. Are your complaints of your supervisors not mostly about their lapses as humans, rather than their lapses as technicians? It is the same for you. The chances are quite good that complaints about you have more to do with how you handle people than prose.

Human beings surround you. They work for you, they work with you and you work for some of them. As an editor, you get work done through people. If you are clumsy with people, it probably hurts your organization more than the graphic artist's clumsiness with her computer.

Skill with people must be your first concern. There are suitable positions in news organizations for people who dislike the subject, but those positions don't bear the title of supervising editor. You must care about people, and learn what you can about what makes them tick.

A key portion of your study of people must be study of yourself. What impact do you have on people? What do they wish you did more of? Did less of? You can find out these things by asking. Your boss will have an opinion, and you should know it.

Yet no one observes you more closely than the people you

supervise, just as you observe your superior closely. We watch those who have power over us, and so your reporters, or photographers, or artists, or copy editors have much to tell you.

You must make your own judgment about the fairness of what you hear. There will be something useful, you can be sure. It may not be expressed as you would express it, it may not feel quite right to you, and yet....

What another person can tell you is what she observes. It will be incomplete. Her gaze does not extend to your interior. You know your good intentions. She knows only what you do and say, and what you do not do and say. And these things she likely sees more clearly than you.

Experiment after experiment, for instance, demonstrates the degree to which people interrupt, and do not realize it. The people being interrupted do realize it. So find ways of asking about your actions, and listen to what you hear.

The wrong way to ask this question, by the way, is to catch someone unawares and pop what will surely feel like a difficult question. If you are going to ask someone for candid words about you, make your request in a thoughtful way and give them time to consider their reply, a day or more later.

Put thought and energy into understanding the people around you, don't take them for granted and form the habit of generosity in your impulses toward them. They deserve the benefit of the doubt until they prove themselves unworthy of it. Your actions should show that assumption of good faith. That goes for your superior, too. After all, if you don't grant it, why should you expect it in return? It is unfair to mistrust your boss just because she is your boss.

The Organization and the Community

Learn more than you should be expected to know about your organization. The invitation here is for you to avoid the easy conclusions that will be offered to you as you settle into your new job.

There will be a conventional line about the circulation department, if you have one, the advertising department and so forth. That conventional line will usually be disparaging. The dynamics of a work group will push you to conform with that conventional opinion. Don't.

It is a bad habit to swallow someone else's judgment without at least chewing a few times. Get to know something about the human resources department before you accept someone else's verdict. What are they proudest of? What are their weak points? What are they doing about these?

Do the same thing with your community. Find ways of learning more than most people would expect you to know. Get out and talk with people, and bring an open mind. You will fill it with fresh information, and have some fun, too.

The staff of a newsroom was in the habit of blaming the conservatism of the community for the distrust in which the liberal newspaper was held. A new editor found something different. The people were quite accepting of the paper's right to its political and social opinions. They just disliked chronic inaccuracy in stories about which they had personal knowledge and felt that the newspaper was generally unwilling to acknowledge its errors.

Accept conventional truth with some reservations. See for yourself. Independent thought is as hard to preserve in a newsroom as in most arenas, and is at least as important.

Strengthening Craft Skills

Any editor will become known for a handful of things, and no more than that. Make one of those things some aspect of the work itself. You cannot be everything, and should not try. But perhaps you are the resident expert on intense interviewing, and everyone knows to turn to you for that. Perhaps you are the queen of the dramatic narrative, and writers with an idea shop their stories to you. Get really good at some aspect of the work, and keep getting better.

The beauty is that you can pretty much choose what you want to be superb at. There are so many things an editor needs to be good at, and no editor is good at all of them. Organizations and bosses tend to know this. So if you are a good supervisor, a good leader and also extremely good at one aspect of the craft, you are in good shape.

Take your pick, and set your standards high. If you want to be the great local government editor, for instance, find out who is the best in the country at shaping coverage of local government. Get to know that person, and pick his brain.

When you became an editor you were good at some aspect of reporting, writing, photography or some other important skill important to your organization. Those abilities helped you to achieve a position of some influence even without an editing title.

Continue learning, for you need knowledge to lead. This does not mean that a director of photography must be the best photographer on the staff, but that he be abreast of developments, techniques and opportunities for his staff, and be curious about many things.

Responsibility for educating yourself comes with your title. A good editor is a student forever.